Table of Contents
What Inspired Me to Write This Collection of Poetry! 4
Chapter One – Who Am I
Who Am I? 6
Poetic 7
Poetry 9
Fallin' Apart!!! 10
Flipping Words 12
My Poetry 15
Every Inch of Me! 16
I Found Opportunities to Explore! 17
Driven 19
I'm Standing on The Pin Head of Success! 22
I'm Hiding 24
Me vs. Me 25
Never Had A Silver Spoon 28
I Saw 30
I Walk on This Land! 31
Death Is Whispering! 32
Chapter Two – Inside My Head
I'm Snapping Photos Inside My Head 34
If God Didn't 36
Why? 37
Always 40
See What I See 41
As The World Turns 42
Peace of Mind 46
What Is Thing Called Life? 48
Stress 49
Moments Captured -N- Time! 51
Inside My Hands! 53
As I Wake ! 54
I Study the Many Faces 55
Walking 57
Ain't It! 58

Some Days 60
Some Days Part Two 62

Some Days Part Three 64
Chapter Three – For the Black Woman
She Is That! 66
I Love You Because 68
Grandpa's Little Girl 69
If I Don't Have You 71
No Storm Can Last Forever 72
To My Unborn Child 74
To My Born Child 75

Birth 76
I Know the Things You've Seen Have Been Cold 77
I Got Lots Of Flowers Today 80
Aborted 83
It's a Baby -N- Her Tummy 86
Suicide 88
Rape 89
Chapter Four – Redemption
Over Nothing! 93
When Will I Smile Again? 96
Sittin' -N- A Cage!! 97
My Generation! 98
Big Words That You Can Understand 100
Talking Inside My Casket 102
Its Happening Too Often 104
I Look In My Young Homies Eyes 107
Urban Ghetto Living 109
Gone With The Wind 111
From The Rooftops 112
The Ghetto 114
Free At Last 116
Wake Up & Stop The Genocide 117
When The Sunshine Turns To Rain 122
I Miss You Momma, I Really Do 124

Chapter One – Who Am I
What inspired me to write this collection of poetry!

My Inspiration

What inspired me was the issues and the things that I see going on in this world today!
Children being raped, molested, and killed
People doing drugs,
People dying from Covid,
Gang members not allowing us that no longer gang bang to step into our hearts and brains in order to change the faulty computer chips that are in there now.
Change has to come, or else my child or your child will be molested, raped,
Or become drug addicts, and or gang members.
I wrote these poems from inside the dirty bowels of Calipatria State Prison, here in California. It blows my mind that I'm able to preach the real and the truth, and also the negative aspects of drugs & gangs & crime to our young youth. But me myself I haven't been able to preach it to myself in order to stay out of prison! It has taken me (20) years to finally wake up and take my head off of this criminal-minded pillow.
I used to think money was everything,
But I'm here to tell that little street hustler,
that it's not, you will get caught sooner or later,
and you will pay dearly
as you sit and rot away mentally and physically in an 8x10 cell.
Wake up like I finally have and find a better way
which is the honest legal way.
God bless the entire world.
I dedicate this poetry and all of my poetry to:
My beautiful wife, Mrs. Tina Bryant.

My grandkids Nhyaree & Tre'von
My sons Jamar & Lil Aaron Jr.
Lovely & Beautiful Daughter Shoska
My daughter Tamarra.
My wonderful mom Mrs. Lucenthia Artis
My mother-in-law Mrs. Joyce Stidum
My Sword & Shield Lonnie LaRae Lucas
All of my family members, brothers, nephews, nieces, aunts, uncles, in-laws,
Tupac Shakur and his mom Mrs. Afini Shakur.
And True Friends
Ya'll know who you are!
One last thing I'd like to say is that over the years I've received a lot of hate from people.
Why? I don't know... But I've done nothing to anyone but show love and keep it real.
I honestly feel this uncalled-for hate is only twisted rages of jealousy which is a waste of time. Get to know me and then I promise you'll love me or learn to respect me and my outlook. I don't hate none of ya'll that hate me, I just ask for you to just let me live.
Peace and Love, from the poet who's waiting to get his chance to flow it..
Aaron Lamar Bryant.....

Who Am I?

There goes the rain
Wetting down all my pain
Seeping life's beautiful substance inside my brain
It's helping the flowers grow
It's helping my outlook on life move calculated and slow
You see I'm trying to understand who I really am
Then once I do, I can explain who I am to them
Metaphors, closed doors Poetry just falling outta my pores
I'm so strong I feel I can walk on water
I feel I can come up with the cure for the Covid slaughter
But I still don't know my true self
I'm fooled as I start to really sink in this water
Trying to protect my health
Breathe
That's what I was told
I'm trying to find out who I am before I become old

Poetic

I'm a poetic mathematician
Taking poetic problems
And knockin' "em" out of commission
Taking cool words, look at how I twist "em" I think it's
special how we're all here
How today we can see the world so clear
And listen to poetry all in our ear
I sometimes wonder when I'll write my last poem
I really can't tell you, I'm just going keep flowin'
I smell warm soup
Another poetic sentence, I'm pushing thru the hoop
That's (2) points for the poetry team Please don't wake me,
I'm diggin' this poetic dream
I see a hand reaching out
Trying to touch me, Man, the hand is telling me to write,
I guess that's God 's plan Days are turning to nights
Nights are turning back into days
Check out the lights
Those are the sunny rays
A good day for you might be a bad day for others
We all come into this world thru our mothers
What if it was the other way around
Your father would be the one to give you birth
How does that sound
Remember we came from the dirt on the ground
Real crazy and whack
But what if that was how life's cycle was really stacked?
Cold question huh Jack?
If everything that is one way now
Could be changed to be the other way around
Do you think you could be on solid ground?
Once again, how does that sound
Let me jump back on track
I'm not trying to trip you out with what I'm saying Because
it's whack

It's just a few crazy poetic thoughts running thru my mind
So I decided to unleash them in this rhyme
I'm a poetic mathematician
Taking poetic problems and
Knockin "em" out of commission

Poetry

My poetry is smooth as glass.
It most definitely has class.
Put it in front of a panel of judges and it'll pass
It's like a compass, it'll help you find your way
My poetry will sit down
And listen to anything you say.
My poetry will even come out of my heart.
And mind to play
Also, my poetry was written to stay.
To stay here
To bring forth a sad or happy tear.
To make someone's life switch a gear.
My words are powerful
Let them kick back inside your ear.
And that's how I'm going to end this poem
My poetry peers!
My Poetry

Fallin' Apart!!!

Somedays I Feel As If I Am Fallin' Apart Unraveling At
My Humanly Seams, Overburdened With All My Worldly
Dreams.
My Mind Seems To Be Sinkin'
Somedays I'm Just Constantly Drinkin' And Two Days
Ago,
I Stayed Up For 48 Hours Just Thinkin' I Wonder If Those
Around Me See What I See? I Wonder If They Are Really
Like Me
I Wonder Are They Fallin' Apart,
Or Are They Standing Strong As A Newborn Tree?
My Mind Feels Like A Driver In The Fast Lane.
That's How It Felt When I Smoked Cocaine.
Just Speeding, Just Going So Fast;
Sometimes I Really Hate To Look Back On My Past;
So Many Broken Memories
That Are Still Hidden Inside A Cast.
My Mind Played Constant Tricks On Me
And Each Time It Did, It Threw It Back In My Face, You
See.
I Cried, I Lied, I Acted Foolish Inside
I Ran From My Problems And Broke Wide,
I Turned To Folks I Knew So I Could Confide.
But They Insulted My Pride,
So I Just Kept Running,
Trying To Find A Place To Hide,
Somedays I Felt Like The Ocean, Wild Crashing Tides.
Lord, Why Am I Fallin' Apart?
Lord, Why Don't I Understand The Things Goin' On Inside
My Heart?
Lord, Why Can't I Laugh, I Can't Smile,
I Can't Dial?
Dial Your Number to Reach

You At Any Hour Of The Day; I Want Life to Be Like My
Young Days, When Me and You Lord Used To Play.
Remember How We Used to
Play Football And Baseball,
How You Would Pick Me Up Lord When I Would Fall
Whisper In My Ear and Tell Me,
You Love Me And To Stand Tall
Lord, Why Are the Pieces Of Me Fallin' Apart?
Is It Because You Want Me to Get Focused And Get
Myself Together,
So That You Can Give Me A Fresh New Start.
I Reach Out to Touch
Nothings There; Just Empty Air,
As I Sit in That Empty Chair,
And Just Look at This Air With An Empty Stare. Why Am
I So Empty? Why Am I So Lost?
I'm Turning to You, Lord
You're My Employer and My Boss.
Settle The Wicked Waves in My Flesh. Help Me Pull
Myself Together, So I Can Pass This Fallin' Apart Test.
There's So Many Pieces of Who I Am,
And Who I Want to Be
Lord, God, Heavenly Father Please Help Me... I'm Fallin'
Apart......

Flipping Words

Transparent I will always be
My poetry is the only thing I want you to see
Sprouting up out of my head like a tree
Unbelievable shine
Unbelievable rhyme
I see 5,000 miles away   little unbelievable children crying
Reason for the tears   they see unbelievable poetry   dying
Check my new picture - check my thought
Concrete creeks   a vision that speaks
A poet who seeks
365-52 weeks
Poetry that leaks   articulation it quietly peeks - traction
I'm rolling thru rain   looking for action
I loved that song "I'm sorry Mrs. Jackson"
My poetic words
I'm seriously waxing
Precision
who was it that made the final decision?
To put Barb Wire around our world and make it a prison!
A timeless work of art
As I sit here and study
and touch it
in the dark

Ghetto and lonely
Lonely and Ghetto
Give me every poem in the world so I can throw "em" and watch "em" settle
Let me snatch the ones written inside of the world's head
Feed "em" - Burp "em" - and then put "em" to bed
Okay   times up
To be a poet - was it meant? - or was it luck?
As I sit here wondering stuck

Poetic style with a new twist, Yeah it was meant No it wasn't luck!
I channel my emotions thru the tip of my pen
I do it from day-2-day-over and over again
Digest the words
Let's both fly like beautiful birds!
Are you curious?
Okay   now get serious!
I made a mental map of my week
I think and come up with poetry
I'm writing in my sleep
I'm torn
Thank you, Mama, Daddy, and God,
And whoever else for letting me be born
Oil, is that the reason our country is warring?
I think it is   my anger is soaring
Let me pull my anger back down to Earth
Study it - hold it - and really look at what it's worth
I am the original blueprint
I am my own government
Look at me, I can't even pay my own rent
The cost of living is too high
We don't own nothing when we die
Look at the real picture
Sitting trapped in the corner of your eye
You can really see it when your eye decides to cry
Lean on my shoulder
Just yesterday - we both got 24 hours   older
As the world didn't get hot
It grew twenty-four degrees colder
I'm coming lukewarm off the press Whole year I've been stressed
Look at my poetry it's half-dressed
Hoping to get a chance to pass the test Thank you, Satan, for letting me be blessed
Did you really understand that last paragraph?
Sit back with me   and add up the math
One plus one   equals two

God didn't let Satan get to me
So my dream came true
That's why today I'm flippin' words at you!
I spin
I deal with the trouble deep within
I grin
I stretch and reach into position
I guess you can say I bend
I also sin   you do it too my friend
No, don't you dare judge
Just sit there   don't even budge
Smell the words - feel the words, hear the words
Be the words, even see the words
That's all I want you to do!
Thank you for letting me flip poetic words at you

My Poetry

Poetry Is Burned
Into My Mind
The Flames Are Roaring
They've Left Behind
A Burned Black Stain
Just Let the Fire
Continue to Burn
Sit Back and Wait
On My Poetry
One Day I'll Get My Turn
My Turn to Let My Poetry Burn
Burn Up Your Head
I Promise You'll Never Forget What ~U~ Read!

Every Inch of Me!

I surrender every inch of me
God, please set me free
Set me free from the sin
That runs deep within that I display again and again.
Set me free from the hate
Do it now, please don't make me wait.
I know U see me standing outside of heavens front gate,
Set me free from doing wrong
Help me do everything to stay focused and strong God, I'm giving you every inch of me God, please set me free. God, do You remember that time We talked by that old oak tree.
My soul was lost.
Every inch of my negative body was tossed.
But God I'm hurting, And I'm tired of paying the cost.
These flames are hot,
Please take me out of hells burning pot.
Earlier in this poem
I thought I was standing outside of Heavens front gate, Oh Wait!
I was just dreaming, please
God make my dreams come true,
because I'm ready to give every inch of me to you.
God please set me free, because now I finally see, What U really want me to be,
As I give you every inch of me.

I Found Opportunities to Explore!

I found opportunities to explore
As the world lets me step my black feet thru its big door
It's more to life than crime
Then dying
Then lying
Then no longer trying
Then crying
It's dreams appearing thru poetry that's rhyming
Thru poetry that's climbing
It's more to life
As I carve across the sky   my future with a sharp knife
Growth potential
Unparalleled visions
I wonder why I've wasted so much time   living inside packed prisons
Finally, my brain is shedding light
I'm expressing what I feel as I sit here and write
This is something I've always wanted to do
My brain is mature
It has finally grew
Before, I didn't have enough courage to try
I really wonder how it would be
On earth if we could really fly
Touch the blue sky   and not die
Fly like a bird
come back to life like Jesus did on the 3rd
The 3rd day gosh I wish life could be lived this way
Finally, for once I'm being heard through little letters
Bunched together called words
Consumed with work
Family pressures
Just a lot of stuff
I wonder am I the main reason my life has been ruff

So tuff
I love life and living & exploring opportunities
I haven't had enough
As I strip down and get naked in front of everybody
And show them I'm buff
Show them my Ghetto elbows and knees that are scuffed
My body is a long 55-year-old story
I'm still reaching for glory
Let go of the fears - let go of the tears
Let the poetry walk slowly thru your ears
I found opportunities to explore
As the world lets me step my black feet thru it's big door!

Driven

Right now, I feel so driven
Driven just like an old rag-a-dee car
Driven like someone or something going too far
I'm driven into a corner driven into a tight ball
I feel like if I get driven anymore, I just might fall I'm driven into a tiny little space
I'm driven and I'm lovin' it can't you see it on my face
Study my driven moods
Study my driven attitudes
I'm tired of the people around me
Being so childish and rude
Look at the gas gauge inside my brain
Its empty and running on "e"
That's why I'm acting so strange/ can't you see I need fuel to run
I need fuel to have fun
I need fuel to shine just like the sun
Lord/why is there so many people that hate me
That wanna shake me
That wanna break me Lord please come and take me
Just take me away
Give me a pair of wings so I can fly today, okay
Just let me soar high
High into the sky
Somedays Lord I'm so driven, I feel like I might die
Lord, I use to run to the drugs to try to escape
My eyes and ears back then were covered with duct tape
But I got right and got back in shape
But Lord I'm driven once again
I'm thinking about making drugs
One more time my best friend
I'm so driven Lord
I know what I'm thinking is a big sin
I'm driven beyond belief
I'm driven and I'm full of grief

I cry out
I've got to keep it real
I need a good dry out
I'm driven and I need to get away from these strange people no doubt
While I'm being driven these are the things I see
These are the things that are killin' me
The cancer-filled cigarettes, secondhand smoke
I don't even know if my lungs tomorrow might be broke
Without them my life's a joke
The drugs/ the lovely crazy thoughts floating thru
These cats' muggs
I just wanna give all these lost souls, a big hug
The hate, the pain
The ugly un-scrubbable stain, such a shame
Everybody around me is smoking Mary Jane
Looking for someone else to blame
They are trying to get away from the madness
They are driven too that's how they deal with the sadness
The deceit, the 120-degree heat
Nobody in this place knows how to stand on their two feet.
I wonder have our intelligent brains been beat.
Beaten by Satan into his submission
Each day/ each other were hating and dissing
Somebody prayed for me
Somebody prayed for all of us
Wake up homie
In God we got to all trust
What's wrong with this world?
Please tell me what's wrong.
We got to get right
God isn't going to let us live like this too long
I'm driven just like a stolen car in a high-speed chase I'm driven into something
My life is shattered like a priceless vase
I'm driven
I'm asking God can I please be forgiven?
I feel so dysfunctional so misunderstood

I wish I could turn into somebody else if I could
I really feel like I'm a million miles apart from myself
And to be truthful it's not healthy for my health
I'm losing' weight pounds just disappearing
I'm driven and myself is what I'm fearing
Those negative voices inside my head
Is what I'm still hearing
I'm driven into a very small ball
God, please hear my desperate call
As I slang this poetry of mines against the wall
Gosh, I'm so driven
As I look at the broken pieces of
this shattered valuable vase
Which is my human face
Let me lay my pen down because I rest my case
I'm driven

I'm Standing on The Pin Head of Success!

I'm standing on the Pin Head of Success
That's where I'm standing, and it feels good to be blessed
I am the ink in the pen that flows
I am the poet Who you will listen to at Poetry Shows
Def Poetry Jam
All over the world spitting poetry at poetry slams
To get where I'm at hasn't been easy or simple
I've been busting Poems out of my head,
Like one would a pimple
Some have been dirty and some have been clean Some Have been nice.
Some have been mean.
Some have been real.
Some have been written like a dream
Guess what world, - I used to be a dope fiend
I smoked cocaine
Let it numb up my brain
Did so much of it, I was able to evade pain
I even fell in the wet rain
Picture that scene inside your brain
I stole, ended up on parole
Been in and out of Prison for thirty-four years
It's finally really taking a toll
I committed bad crimes
Back then, I wasn't thinking about writing rhymes
I needed money
I didn't care if it came to me in… Nickels and Dimes
I hurt people
I lied to people
I cried with people
I knew these people
These people were my family and friends

When I was down and out,
I could go to them and get some ends
You see, one day I finally woke up and peeped the game I
realized I wanted to be different and not the same.
I realized I wanted to use my brain
The one thing inside my body
That's as powerful as a train
So I jumped on the right set of tracks
Peeped all the poetic facts
And told myself I wanna touch everybody in the heart
From whites, Asians, Mexicans, and blacks
I wanna smell success
I wanna pass life's difficult, but passable test
I wanna finally be blessed
No longer stressed
My negative side was laid to rest
Look at the head of this pen,
You can stand on it with me to my friend
It's strong, it won't bend
Here give me your hand, I'll pull you up here
Together we can shed a happy and successful tear
Write poetry together, and stuff it into the world's ear
I'm so hungry, I've eaten everything on the plate
Show me love world, please don't show me hate
God gave me the keys to success last night at his front gate
It feels good up here on the head of this pen
I'm standing on the pen head of success and that's how I
want this poem to end.

I'm Hiding

I'm hiding behind and in between my sentences and words
I'm hiding in the ghetto, with all the lost Ghetto birds

I'm hiding in my poems
I'm hiding when I flow "em" When I throw "em"
And when I show "em"
It feels good to hide
Hide on the side, hide on the tide
Hide inside my tears that I cried
Hiding behind myself as I break wide
Hiding as I slip & slide
Hiding behind my own pride
Hiding behind all the times when I lied
Hiding behind all the times
I hurt those I love deep down inside
I'm hiding inside my own head
I'm hiding underneath my Ghetto bed
I'm hiding behind the colors blue and red
Hiding because I don't wanna end up dead
I'm hiding behind a Ghetto trash can
I'm hiding behind that mask again
I wanna stop hiding from all these things I spoke of
I'm tired of hiding from the man up above
I'm tired of hiding, so please world show me love

Me vs. Me

I always prayed for what didn't happen to me,
For it to happen
It's okay poetry world, you can start clapping
Let me tell you what's happening'
Well it's the SHO-down, and here we both are
Aaron against his other half, a spirit named Star   Aaron:
"Hey Star?" Star:
"Yeah, Aaron what's going down?" Aaron:
"Hey bro, let's have a seat right here on the ground.
I must let you know what I'm going thru.
So listen up because this poetic conversation everything
being said is true.
I wanna kill you Star
I think you're trying to kill me.
I think if I kill you Star, then I'll finally be free.
Free from the pain.
Free from the game.
Free from all this shame.
Bring me in from the rain"
"Hey Star, I think you're trying to set me up, Wet me up,
and never let me up.
Hey Aaron, that's not even right.
I'm your spirit, and I want you to shine like a light,
Real bright.
Never dull or low, this is the SHO-down fo-sho.
Hey Star,
Why do you make me think about doing evil stuff?
Why do you make me act hard and tuff?
Star, stop okay, because I've had enough.
Hey Star, why did you make me go out and commit crime?
And you knew I was going to get caught And do a gang of
time." Star:
"Well Aaron, I was going thru some things too.
I was battling you Aaron, and I didn't know what to do.
I thought you were trying to do me in.

I swear to God,
It didn't seem like you were even being my friend.
You were hanging around people I didn't even like, Aaron.
I tried to holler at you,
It seemed like you weren't even caring.
Wasn't doing any sharing.
Look at ourselves, sitting here just staring.
Staring at ourselves destroying each other's health.
Spying on each other like the spy plane called the stealth."
Aaron:
"Hey Star, what are we going do about all this trippin'?
About us both slippin'?
You were the one that had me crippin.'
Look at Mama,
Tears falling from her pretty eyes, Just drippin'." Star:
"Hey Aaron, I guess all we can do is fight each other.
Whoever wins can then get rid of the other, Or we can settle
our differences and speak and shake hands my brother."
Bam! Bam! Bam!
Aaron hits star
Star feels like he was hit by a speeding car, And feels punch
drunk as if he drank ten drinks at the bar.
Star shakes it off and comes back swinging nice and swift.
Catches Aaron across the jaw and Aaron starts to drift.
Drift out into the street,
Losing step with his own feet,
But he regains his balance and gets his vision straight,
And sees his little granddaughter
Standing in the front yard at the gate.
She yells out "Grandpa -papa!
Why are you fighting your own flesh and blood?" Aaron:
When I hear this, I feel like my whole body was stuck in
mud, lost in crud
I yell out to Star, and tell him this has got to stop
Share-with-me-the-number-to-this combination lock
Let me open the me-vs me door
Let me get help from you
To stop this mental and physical war

My brain and body are sore
Everything is hurting to the core
As I listen to imaginary waves
Crashing against my heart's shore
I'm like a piece of paper that's tore
Star starts to cry
I feel the tears because they are falling out of my eye Star:
Star says "Aaron, I love you, bro, let's get back on track." I apologize for the times I forced you to do crack.
I apologize for the times I made you act foolish, black,
And even the times when
I made you think you were a
Mack,
I apologize to you for the times I turned on you my back."
Aaron:
"Hey Star, I'm sorry for all the dirt I've done.
All I wanna do is finally love you and have fun.
Shine bright just like the sun."
So Star and Aaron embrace
Look each other deep in the face
Thank you God-for-this-mirror in-my-hand
It wasn't a waste
As Star and Aaron dust off, and get back on pace Me vs. Me
Poetry straight lace.

Never Had A Silver Spoon

I never had a silver spoon
In the Ghetto as a little kid
I had so many dreams -N- my bedroom
When I came outside,
It felt like I just stepped outta a cocoon
Went down the street one day
And all my innocence was tossed up to the moon
The next day I hit the block and dove into the crack game
Like one would into a swimming pool, full bloom
SPLASH
Damn it's a trip to sit here and reflect back on my past
I never had a silver spoon
I wish I could rewind time back and reach up and take my
innocence back down from the moon
I wish I had of spent my free time more wisely
I can hear my daddy playing the greatest hits by the Isleys
The 60's, The 70's, The 80's, The 90's
Shit it's Damn near 2023
As I sit here writing this poem, tripping off myself you see
Just let me go back and forth in time
and please do your best to understand my thoughts
In this Poetry I'm droppin' that rhymes
A lot of my friends lied
A lot of 'em' died
I'm gonna keep it real with you
Only for some of them I cried
I wonder who's gonna cry,
when I twist and walk off this earth,
I wonder what all my written Poetry is gonna be worth
I smell Ghetto Meals
I seek Ghetto Thrills
I was involved in ghetto dope deals

I did drugs, and I swallowed certain types of "get high off of them" pills
Asl hustled, stole, and robbed, to get me a nice set of wheels
What did I accomplish? what did I gain?
Fucked it off in puffs of addictive cocaine
such a shame
Guess what? I never even reached Fame
Still representing my ghetto street given name
I don't want the name no more
I wanna throw it in the trash as I exit outta the street life's
"back door"
It's too many people peeking
It's too many people speaking
In my eyez
Everyone of "em's" brains is leaking
As I look up and still see my innocence,
Sitting up on the moon.
I never had a silver spoon

I Saw

I Saw a Chair with No Table
I Saw a T.V. With No Cable
I Saw a Hat with No Head
I Saw a Tool with No Shed
I Saw a Pillow with No Bed
I Saw a Foot with No Shoe
I Saw an Apartment with Rent That's Due
I Saw a Picture with No Frame
I Saw a Person Who Couldn't Read or Write; Or Remember
Their Own Name
I Saw Some Soap with No Dish
I Saw a Fish Tank with No Fish
I Saw a Fight with No Punches
I Saw a School Cafeteria with No Lunches
I Saw a Family with No Home
I Saw All This as I Sat Here and Wrote This Poem

I Saw

I Walk on This Land!

I walk on this land!
And each day I do it as a Black man
I crunch the gravel famous folks kicked up before I walk
through the Ghetto
Sometimes my own people are the ones who won't
Open a happy door
Everyday life is just like a war
And each day my brain is deeply sore
Somedays it's hard to even talk
Somedays all I do is just get up and walk
I walk on this land
And each day I do it as a Black man
I walked a thousand miles yesterday
Walked up on some happy Whites
And they wanted to play
We laughed, we talked, we walked, we cried together
Because they felt my being Black pain
And they told me, hey we aren't the same
But that don't mean we can't get to know each other's name
And help each other acquire fame
Pull each other through
Our moments when we feel ashamed
So, we exchanged numbers, names, and addresses
Threw away our stresses
Asked God if He bless us
And I started to walk home
Because I walk on this land
And each day I do it as a Black man

Death Is Whispering!

Death Is Whispering Inside My Ear.
It's Telling Me That It Wants to Come Get Me.
Later This Year.
I Start Crying Like a Very Emotional Person,
Then I Play Tuff with Death and Start To Cursin'.
I Look Deep into My Salty Tears.
Inside "Em" I See All My True Fears
I Step Back.
I Ask "Death" Why Is He Coming at Me Like That?
He said,
"I've Been Chasing You Since You Were Born Black."
I Feel "Death" Touch My Skin.
I See "Death" Trying to Act Like He's My Friend.
I See "Death" Trying to Kill Me Once Again.
I Smell Something It's "Death."
I Gotta Fight Back, I Can't Let Him Steal My Breath!
Death Is Well Lubricated,
As He Takes A Swing At My Head.
He Whispers Once Again,
Tells Me, He Wants Me Dead.
I Start Running Real Fast,
As "Death" Is Chasing Me, Having A Blast.
It's Scary Because He's Hiding Behind an Ugly Mask
He Tells Me You Can't Get Away
He Said If I Can't Get You Now, I'll Get You Another Day
I Stop and Turn Around
I Hold My Ground
I Tell "Death" I'll Get Down With -U- Pound -4- Pound
So We Both Put Up Our Dukes And Throw Blows
I Break "Death's" Nose. Stomp On His Black Rose,
And I Rip Up A Few Pieces of His Clothes.
"Death" Hits Me with A Stiff Left.
Tries To Reach into My Soul…
Once Again to Steal My Breath.
We Fall to The Ground and Continue To Tumble.

Rumble…We Get Up and Once Again Stumble
Now We're Mixed Up, And Hot,
Like A Pot of Seasoned Gumbo
Death Is Whispering -N- My Ear
As I Wake Up from This Crazy Dream
And I Finally See Life Very Clear
I Really Wonder About "Death"
And I Do Realize That One Day I Will Have to Take My
Final Breath
I Wish I Could Die And Then Just Come Back
Wouldn't It Be Cool If I Could Do That?
As I Still Hear Death Whispering Behind My Back

P.S. I Wonder How Many Times I'll Beat Death Up
Before He Finally Beats Me Up!!!

Chapter Two – Inside My Head
I'm Snapping Photos Inside My Head

My brain is like a camera with a bright flash
The photo is captured and frozen of what just happened
And, what happened in the past
I see throwback jerseys and tight baseball caps
Photos snapped of me and my old dead friends, playing on
The railroad tracks
I see metaphors of war
Photos snapped of people in this country hungry and poor
I picture Chicago Cabrini green
Photos snapped of me and the president of the United
States in a dream
I see a photo of a pair of faded jeans with an irregular seam
I also see a photo of a
Dope dealer balancing his future on a triple beam
Flashes from the camera jumping all thru my mind
I see a photo inside my head of Martin and Malcolm dying
I also see a photo of their wives crying
I see a photo of a cloud of pain
My camera didn't flash this time
It got wet from the rain
It still snapped the picture, of my
Black race lost smoking crack cocaine
I see a photo of somebody in the wrong place
I'm studying this picture, but I don't recognize their face
I see a photo of someone lying in a casket
Some days I feel like laying in it with them.
Life is so drastic
I see a photo of someone sitting at home
Cold thing though, they got no thoughts running through
Their dome
I see a photo of a book with missing pages

I also see a photo of a prisoner with life, mind going thru cold stages
I see a photo of Jam Master Jay
I see a photo of me changing
Everything that happened that day
I see a photo of me saving his life
I see a photo of me having dinner
With his son's, family and wife
I'm snapping photos inside my head
And I'm looking at the photo of me writing this poem
While I sit on my prison bed
I see pictures inside my head
Of what I think GOD looks like
I see a photo of myself as a kid riding on my first bike
I see photos of people in heaven,
Some in Hell
I see photos of poets in the world with a story to tell
Why am I seeing all these photos
All these pictures All these visions
I see a photo of doctors cutting open a human body
Making a life-or-death decision
I see a photo of me bringing this poem to a close right here
Trapped inside this prison
My brain is like a camera with a bright flash
The photo is captured and frozen of what just happened and what happened in the past

If God Didn't

If God Didn't
Want Me To Cry
Then He Wouldn't Have Given Me Tears If God Didn't
Want Me To Hear
Then He Wouldn't Have Given Me Ears If God Didn't
Want Me To See
Then He Wouldn't Have Given Me Eyes Don't You Agree
If God Didn't
Want None Of This To Come True
Then He Wouldn't Have Created Me & You

Why?

I wonder why?
Why I am one of the few that can see this world? Thru my eye
Why do twisted things make us all cry? Why is this world the way it is?
Why is there someone out there Lurking and hiding?
Killing and molesting our kids?
Why is there a big blue sky?
Why do regular people have to pass away?
I really wonder why?
Why are drugs being sold?
Why does my body grow old?
Why does the weather change From warm to cold?
Why is this 'wanna-be tuff' guy Acting so bold?
There's a story behind him That needs to be told.
Why do people lose their mothers? Why do people lose their families?
Fathers, sisters, and brothers?
Why are so many people lost?
Emotions tossed,
Outlooks on life ex'd out and crossed?
Why aren't people being found?
Why don't people hear a sound?
Why does dirt need to be in the ground?
Why is what I wanna know?
Why are some people rich and some po?
As we sit back and watch the world spin slow?
Why do people fight,
Write, get uptight?
Why does this stuff go on?
Every day and every night?
Why do people play?
Why do people hate people that are gay? What if you had of ended up that way?

Why do people judge
Hold a grudge,
Know their wrong   and don't wanna budge? Why are people fat? Black, not intact, On crack?
Why are people skinny?
Greedy when they already have plenty,
People in Africa don't have any?
Why? I ask As I look up into the sky,
As a teardrop falls from my eye.
Why do people spread false rumors?
Why do people get tumors?
Why are some people late bloomers?
Why do people not bathe?
Misbehave?
Why did people have to slave?
Why is that 5-year-old child buried in that grave?
Why don't some people eat?
Don't have shoes on their feet?
Don't live in a house with water or heat?
Why does a woman stay -n- a relationship   Where she always gets beat?
Why? I don't understand the mistreat.
Why do some people die so tragic?
Why don't some people perform magic?
Why?
I didn't invent that million-dollar gadget?
Why can a plane fly?
Why have some planes fallen out of the sky?
Tell me God why
Did those people on September 11th have to die? As I set this poem down and hold my tears back
I wanna cry.
Why?

Always

Always
The world wakes up to what we call days
Always
We search for the sun to enjoy the rays
Always
I sit back and I study my humanly ways
Always
I trip when I hear people hate and talk about gays
Always
It hurts my heart when I think about those who had to slave
Always
We find ourselves running from the rain
Always
We look and listen to the thoughts inside our brain
Always
We find ourselves not understanding why we have to experience pain
Always
Another child is born
Always
Another person's heart is torn
Always
Our souls are soaring
Always
There's something going on
Always
There's someone weak and someone strong

See What I See

See what I see
Then maybe you might agree with me
Judges and mayors smoking crack
Mayor Marion Berry, am I speaking a fact?
They feel what we feel
I wonder are these feelings fake. Or are they real?
They get sexual urges they come forth in a moment of lust
President Clinton did it, trust I'm not trying to be X-rated
I'm just keeping you updated
See what I see
Then maybe you might agree with me
You see We trust our kids in these churches with the priest
But he's the one molesting us at the least
I wonder when these crazy times are gonna cease
Look at me, I'm throwing up to you the sign peace
It's not a gang sign Sit there and think about all those Ghetto mama's crying
Their young babies out in the streets dying
The system giving up on "em" No Longer Trying They lock up gang members for gangbanging
But what about the police they doing the same thing
Hanging and nicknaming
Not all of us Ghetto kids are evil and wrong
Not all the police are out to pick a bone
All of us that are righteous Let's help those who are corrupt get back strong
See what I see Because it's all been going on far too long
See what I see
Then maybe you might agree with me
The last thing I wanna speak about is Covid, Cancer, and Aids
They say that it's not man-made
Then why wasn't it here back during the Biblical days? Sex has been on this earth since the earth started

Is it really population control?
I'm broken-hearted
Just think they blame anal sex on gays
But they ain't the only ones practicing anal sex these days
Or even back in the biblical days
Look at the picture within the picture Can you see that picture?
This deadly virus was brewed up in a lab
And they wonder why I'm sitting here mad
Do you see what I see?
Then if you do, step over here and let the wind blow free
Because now we both agree

As The World Turns
Part Two

As the world turns
My cold calculated mind continues to burn
There's a lot of stuff I don't understand
Like the fact that I was born a Black Man
Sometimes I sit back and think about changing colors
From Black 2 White
I wonder then, would things in my life,
Finally go right I also wonder; would I be able to still write
Write poetry that's airtight
Just thank
A bullet is hitting somebody in the head, point blank
As the world turns
That bullet is wiping out their memory bank
Also, there's a teenager sipping on his first drank
Right now, somebody is giving up on life
Also, there's somebody in the hospital not wanting to die, up under the knife
Listen to the quiet laughter
I wonder if the book of our lives is in the last chapter
Rewind life
And this time really read the pages
Life is a trip, as we trip off the many stages
As the world turns
These tears in my eyes make my eyes really burn
Ain't this a trip
We all came from a little drop of sperm
Sperm is some powerful stuff
There's a lot of it in this world,
But I wonder is it's enough?
Reproduction
Another human life created,

Due to a moment of raw seduction
I just wanna scream
AHHGGH!!!
As the world turns
I wonder is this really reality
Or is it really a dream? Hush, Sssh there's no rush
Who invented cuss words?
Who invented all the beautiful birds?
Was it God, or was it something or somebody,
We don't know
Sit back and watch the world turn, real slow
I wish I could just walk to the top of the earth
Watch me be born, and say I witnessed my own birth
Is death like birth? Because at birth,
We don't even remember coming into this earth
Is birth like death?
We relocate because someone else requires our breath.
As the world turns
Why do people cry?
Get high?
Wish they could fly?
But never try?
Cold thought and questions, hanging in the sky
I wanna cut the world in half
Add and subtract people like 5th-grade math
Then sit back and only laugh
I want those who live comfortably
To live in the streets
No shoes or socks on their feet
Laid out on cookie sheets
(Life's cold treats)
Please help me I'm cold
As the world turns
Each day we're getting old
Place me and my soul in a warm home
And let me watch the moon turn inside my dome
Why do people rape?
Just hearing about it, bends me out of shape

Gosh I wish I could just escape
Escape to another zone
As the world turns
They're in a lab trying once again to clone
Is it right, or is it wrong?
Family's falling apart Cocaine, Meth, and Heroin
Tearing out a mother's heart I feel like a ship that's sinking
I feel like a person who's drinking
I feel like a person on death row, seriously thinking
As the world turns
My mind continues to burn
And my heart continues to yearn
I see a hungry child reaching their hands out for food
I see the government harboring it Issuing it out in small
clumps, with an attitude
Why is the world so unequal?
Why are life's movements
Set up to look just like a movie sequel?
So much is unfair OOPS, there grows another gray hair
Is it wisdom or stress?
The world is steady turning
And I wanna understand this test
As the world turns
Will I ever be blessed?
I'm thinking about all the people who stepped
Into this earth before I did
Now I'm thinking about all those who stepped out of it
While I was growing up as a kid What's the meaning?
Why is everybody constantly dreaming
Why is that crazy person in a mental hospital Hollering and
Screaming
As the world turns
I wonder are they a demon
Who brought me here? Who's voice was the first one I heard
in my little ear?
Was it my father and mother?
Or was it some other?
Look at your entire family tree

It all-began-somewhere-don't-you-agree
As the world turns
And we sit on top of this tree I wanna see things that no one
Else has ever seen
I don't care if their dirty or clean I don't even care if their
evil or mean I don't even care if it's real or all a big dream
As the world turns
My mind continues to burn
Respect where you came from
It was from a beautiful drop of sperm.

Peace of Mind

Will my peace of mind come when I'm dying?
Will it be while I'm crying?
Or will it come while, my eyes are dying?
I remember a talk I had with Grandpa
Let me tell you about it as I lean my back against this wall.
You see, he asked what I wanted outta life
I told him, a brand-new Cadillac,
pockets full of money, and a fine wife.
I told him I wanted jewelry and cars
I wanted to step out on the town, with all the movie stars.
I told him I wanted to consume expensive drinks, in the neighborhood bars.
You see, I didn't really understand what he asked
All I was concerned about was having a blast
He told me son, that's not what I mean.
Wake up, sit up straight, and snap outta that dream.
I said, "well grandpa, what are you saying?"
As I listened to him,
And the Isleys on the record player playing.
He said all I want outta life is a peace of mind.
I looked deep into grandpa's eyes
And I knew he wasn't lying.
He said; inner peace, peaceful thoughts,
No more stumbling blocks, no more peeking over my shoulder as I hear gunshots!
No more moments of anger
No more days living life as a stranger
No more days being like a good shirt with no hanger
No more pain no more bad days getting wet from the rain
No more doing silly thangs
That make me look a damn shame
Just peace just beautiful relaxing times

No more stressing worrying about if I'm dying
No more people running up to me with bad news
No more being a ghetto detective trying to piece together the bad clues
As un-peaceful moments' walk around with me, inside my pair of crooked shoes.
Just peace
All drama and negativity put to a cease.
Grandson
Let me ask you again,
As he reached out and touched my face and chin
And smiled at me and made me grin
What do you want outta life?
"Grandpa, I want nothing but peace.
That's all I want at the least.
As I said a prayer to God as I faced the middle east
Just nothing but raw moments filled with peace!!"

Dedicated to every grandfather and grandson in this Entire World....

What is This Thing Called Life?

Somebody Tell Me What It Is?
Or What It Be....
Life, Am I Supposed to Feel Free?
Or Is It Something That I'm Supposed to See?
Who Is It That Blew Breath into My Body.
To Let Me Finally Breathe?
Who Is It That Takes That Final Breath from Our Bodies,
And Tells Us It's Time to Leave?

Can Someone Answer?
Who Is It That Created Cancer?
What Is a Brain? What Is Pain?
What Is a Name? What Is Rain?
Why Into This World We Came?
Why Come Some People Act the Same?
Why Come Some People Act Strange?

I Got a Lot of Questions: And I'm Gonna Keep Asking.
Tell Me Why Is Everybody Laughing?
Life Is It Funny?
Life Is It Worth More Than Money?
Life....
What Is Life?
Tell Me What It Is.
Or What It Be?
Because Life,
I Finally Wanna Understand You See.

Stress

Folds Of Cigarette Smoke.

Inside My Pockets Are Books of Poetry That I've Wrote

I Smell the Air.

My Whole Life I Lived It on A Dare.

As I Rewind My Personal Thoughts Back Inside My Head,

And Sit Down on This Chair.

Who Made This Chair?

Who Sat It Right There? I Wonder Was It Fair?

You See I Study Life, I Study Strife.

I Also Carve It Away With A Knife.

I Wanna Understand

This Whole Thing Called Living, Giving.

Who Was It That Invented the Ribbon?

Who Invented Laughter?

Just Last Night I Wrote a Book,

It Started And Ended in One Chapter.

Why Do We Read? Bleed? Not Take Heed?

Poetry I'm Trying to Feed.

Feed To Your Heart and Brain.

Why Are People Abusing Their Bodies with Cocaine?

Sending It Thru Numbed Up Pain.

Pushing It To The Edge Trying to Make It Snap Like a
Bicycle Chain, Inhale Exhale,
Now Let Your Mind Picture Jail.
Let Your Mind Picture When U Used to Walk to School
with A Lunch Pail.
Now Let Your Mind Picture A Place Called Hell.
Somebody Lean Over and Knock the Dust Off My Chest.
Because I'm Too Tired, I Need to Rest.
I Just Pray I Can Pass This Poetry Test.
God Bless,
Please Drain My Body of All This Wicked Stress!

Moments Captured -N- Time!

So Sit Back And Enjoy This Poetry I'm Spitting At You
With A Rhyme
Rodney King Being Beaten Down
Batons Hitting Flesh and Bone
Listen To the Sound
Stand Up Firm and Hold Your Ground
Moments Captured -N- Time
John F. Kennedy Being Shot and Dying
That Whole Day the World Was Crying
Or How About the First Man on The Moon
Or How About That Pretty Butterfly
Flying Outta That Cocoon
Study The Last Picture of Tupac Before He Died
Tell Me World How Did You Feel Inside?
Malcolm X Being Shot
The Video Is in Stores | It Can Be Bought
As I Sit Here Shaking, Hurt, Pissed Off and Hot
Pictures Of Little White Kids and
Black Kids Playing Together
Pictures Of Thunderstorms,
And Hurricanes Tearing Up Stuff
What's Up with The Crazy Weather
Pictures Of Folks We Love Dying of Covid,
Don't Forget A.I.D.S.
Pictures Of The Police Busting in Houses Pulling Raids
Pictures Of Monkey Pox,
And The Relative That Got Shot!
Is This Shit Really Real That We See?
Blasting Across Social Media And Tv?
Who Was the Person Who Created Film & Photos?

Shit It's Now Digital,
Moments Captured -N- Time?
I Think About This All the Time.
Flo Jo Photographed Running Track
I Wonder Why She Had to Die | Black
Pictures Of Columbine
Pictures Of Students Crying - Some Dying
You Saw the Pictures Too, | I Ain't Lying
Pictures Of Stars Falling
Pictures Captured in Time Of Hungry Children Calling
Pictures Of Michael Jordan Balling
Pictures Of Me Inside My Casket Sleeping
Pictures Of My loved One's Peeping
Pictures Of a Lost Soul's Brain Seeping
Seeping Into a Ghetto Street
Pictures Of a Black Child Shackled at The Feet
Pictures Of U.S. Currency Rolling Off the Sheet
Pictures Of Life Looking Real Sweet
Moments Captured -N- Time
Pictures Of Humans Robbing Banks for Money
I Wonder Why This Is a Crime?
They Needed the Money for A Reason
A Moment Captured -N- Time
Is Me Sitting Here Smiling and Cheesing
A Moment Captured -N- Time
Was The Real Picture Snapped of All of Ya'll Listening
To My Poetry with A Rhyme!
That Was a Moment Captured -N- Time

Inside My Hands!

Is A Set of Palms | Full of Tears
Palms Full of My Deepest Darkest Fears
Palms Full of Different Voices | I'm Hearing in My Ears
Inside My Hands
I Throw My Pain Around
Pick It Back Up Off the Ground
Throw It Out to Sea
And Watch It Silently Drown
Inside My Hands
Is a Lot of Anger
A Lot of Force
I've Used My Hands So Much | That Their Like Nappy Hair
Hard & Course
Inside My Hands
Are Beautiful Faces
People I Know
That Are in Different Places,
and They All Are Different Races
Inside My Hands
There Sits a Fighter
Also There Sits a Poetry Writer
Trying To Use His Hands to Make His Poetry Tighter
As I Light the Whole Poetry Game Up with This Lighter
Inside My Hands
Is A Lot of Understanding
Sometimes My Hands | Have Been Quite Demanding
Inside My Hands
There's A Lot of Dreams
As I Post Up My Poetry with My Hands/All Over the World
As Funny as That Seems
Inside My Hands - I'm Molding Together All My Plans

As I Wake!

As I Wake
My Thoughts Start to Break
Break -N- Half
As I Start to Painfully Laugh
I Wonder How Many People Died Last Night
Cried Last Night –
And Even Found a Place to Hide Last Night
Just Sit There and Think
Let Your Thoughts Break Away from Your Memory Bank
How Rich Are Your Thoughts
When -U- Get Full of That Drank?
My Past Keeps Tapping Me on My Shoulder
As I Wake, I'm Getting Older and Older
Touch Air - Is Your Life Going Pretty Fair?
As We Sit (5) Hundred Miles Apart and Just Stare
As I Wake
I Silently Shake
I Listen to My Bones | As It Sounds Like They Break
But They Only Poppin - Back into Place
As I Look at The Clock of Life's Face
It's Telling Me A Time
It's Listening to The Thoughts on My Mind
As I Sit Here and Write Poetry with A Rhyme
As I Wake
I Picture Me Walking Across a Shallow Lake
I Picture Me Blowing Candles Out On Someone Else's Cake
I Think About Life - I Wonder Is It Real or Fake?
I Really Wonder as I Wake
And Also, As I Watch My Thoughts Silently Break
As I Wake

I Study the Many Faces

I Study the many faces
Worldwide they've been to many places
Some faces are left out -n- the snow
Some faces are still trying to grow
Some faces are old and slow
Some faces are left out -n- the sun
Some faces are full of joy and fun
Some faces are hiding from someone

I see a face something like yours
I look deep into it's pores
And I see all the facial wars
So elegant, so different, So Black
You've seen slavery days front your face and it's a fact
The moments when it was mad
Sad, then brick glad
The smiles, the tears, the fears.
And I see what this face has went thru over the years
Some faces are tuff
Some are soft & not ruff
Some faces don't have enough
Something's missing, something should be there
As I sit here
And at your beautiful missing something face
I just stare
And smell the wisdom from your gray hair
I see a fare coming in from the rain
I see a face so numb from cocaine
From shame
From blame
The face has attached to it a name
I wonder what it feels

And why it continues to send itself thru cheap thrills
I see a face that's lost
But is soon to be found
I still see my grandmother's beautiful face 6 feet underground
So beautiful as the days when she was here
Excuse me I gotta quickly shed a tear
I study the many faces
And looking at "em"
I can tell they've been to many places
I study the many faces

Walking

Walking alone on a crowded street~
Lost in thought looking at my feet~
Cutting up poetry like cookies on a sheet~
Body and emotions so tired and beat ~
A piece of candy in my mouth so sour; not even sweet~

Walking to a place where time flows~
Walking to a place where nobody even wears clothes~
Walking to a place where my brain slowly grows~
Walking to a bad place but I never made it
Because my body froze~

Walking in a tight little space~
Footsteps and footprints walked, look back, there's not even a trace~
Look at my walk~ study my walk~
Now do my walk~
Do it silently ~ don't you even talk~
I'm just walking alone on a crowded street~
Lost in thought looking at my feet~
Enjoying this thang called poetry~
Damn it's so sweet!
Just walking looking down at my feet...

Ain't It?

Ain't It Beautiful and Ain't It a Trip
That We Are Really Here on Earth
Ain't It a Trip
That the World Really Had Our Birth
Ain't It
What Are We Really? Are We Human?
Are We Something Else?
Are We Computers with Flesh Covering Them Like Car Covers
Are We Really Sisters - Fathers - Mothers - Uncles - Aunties Grandkids - And Brothers
Ain't It a Trip
Ain't It a Trip How the Ocean Is There
Ain't It a Trip to Just Sit Back and Stare
Ain't It a Trip How We Grow Hair
Ain't It
Ain't It a Trip How We Can Talk – Walk
and Then One Day When Life Ends Our Spirit Is Then Outlined In Chalk
Where Do We Really Go When It's Done Here
Ain't It a Trip How Everyone Can Shed a Tear
Ain't It a Trip How Some of Us Can't Even See or Hear
Ain't It a Trip How Some People Can Bring Fear
Ain't It a Trip How You Can Love Someone So Close and Dear
Look At the Moon and The Stars
Ain't It a Trip How We Can Drive Around the World Inside Of Cars
Ain't It a Trip How We Can Write
and Also How the World Goes to Sleep at Night
Ain't It a Trip How Water and Dirt Makes Mud

Ain't It a Trip That in Order for Us to Live Our Bodies
Need Blood
and A Lot of Love - So That We Can Bud
And Also Bloom
Ain't It a Trip How N.A.S.A. Can Send People Up to The
Moon
Ain't It a Trip That We Can Do So Many Thangs
Ain't It a Trip That We Can't Find the Solution to Make Our
Youth Stop Wanting to Bang
Ain't It
Ain't It a Trip That I Can Choose Right Now to Bring This
Poetry to A Close
as I Drop It Outta My Hands as You Remember My Final
Pose
Ain't It a Trip

Some Days

Some Days;
I find it hard to mellow out and relax
Some Days;
I wish I could remind my life back to a little kid and play
with jacks
Some Days;
I get weird attitudes that I don't understand
And I really wonder what's wrong with myself man.
Some Days;
I wonder when I'm going to die
Some Days;
I really wonder about this and I just start to cry
Some Days;
I just wish I could get away from the earth and walk up into
the sky
Some Days;
I just wanna tell everybody bye
I feel this way because I don't think they see
This world the same way
Through my eyes
Some Days;
I just wanna scream
Some Days;
I wonder if this thing called life
Is one big dream
Some Days;
That's what it seems
Some Days;
I just want to go and wake up the dead
And let them all paint a vivid picture of what death is like
inside my head Some Days;
I just feel like I'm going crazy

I just feel so lazy
Some Days;
I question who my friends really are
Some Days;
I feel as if I'm trapped inside a jar
Some Days;
I just wanna let go of all the things I'm holding on to
Some Days;
I just feel out of touch with you and you
Some Days;
I just don't have any thoughts to share
Some Days;
I just feel like no one around me even cares
Some Days;
I feel like I wanna stop climbing
Up life's set of difficult stairs Some Days;
I just snapped back
Some Days;
I just feel I have to write a poem like that!

Some Days Part Two

Some Days;
I just sit back and watch the world spin
Some Days;
I really wonder about the day this all began
Some Days;
I trip off really being here
Being able to see things so clear
Being able to really hear
Some Days;
I just would like to sit at the very bottom
Of someone else's ear
Some Days;
I would like to stroll quietly through someone's salty tears
Some Days;
I find myself searching for an answer
Some Days;
I sit back and really trip off HIV and cancer
Somedays
I wonder where these things started
Some Days;
I look at this twisted world and I become broken hearted
Some Days;
I take a real hard look at our troubled youth
Some Days;
They frustrate me so much
I just want to go through the roof
Some Days;
You feel the same way
So you know I'm telling the truth
Some Days;
I wish I could bring back some of those who are dead
Some Days;
I wish I could let you have a full day to sit inside my head
I wonder if you've even heard

Anything I've ever said
Some Days;
I wonder how I'm really going to go Some Days;
I wake up and walk through the day real slow and Some Days;
I just have to write a poem like this
With a smooth flow

I dedicate this poem to my brother Alvin Jr.

Some Days Part Three...

Some Days;
I wake up and I think about who left this earth last night
Some Days;
I think about all the stuff around me that isn't right
Some Days;
I wonder why I get so mad and I just wanna fight
Some Days;
I get focused and I grab my pen to write
Some Days;
God grabs me and shines on me His bright light
Some Days;
I crawl right into the center of that thing called hate,
Some Days;
I just wanna vanish from this state
Some Days;
I just wanna rewind this world back to the biblical days
Some Days;
I really wonder why so many people dislike gays
Some Days;
I wonder if you end up like them
Would you change your funny ways?
Some Days;
I feel people should just mind their own
Some Days;
If you really look at it you might just live real long
Some Days;
My body feels strong and not weak
Some Days;
I just can't even find the words to speak
Some Days;
I just wanna love the world
Would that make me a freak?
I just wanna ride the bus
Some Days;
I just feel like I'm losing everybody's trust

Some Days;
I feel myself running my fingers through the dust
Some Days;
I find myself looking at everything with raw lust
Some Days;
I feel like I'm losing my mind
Some Days;
I just feel like busting up laughing
Instead of crying
Some Days;
I just wish I could be the tallest tree
Some Days;
I just ask God to set me free
Some Days;
I just have to write a poem like this!
Some Days

Chapter Three – For the Black Woman
She Is That!

She Is That
She Is That Black Woman
Black As Night
Black And Clearly in My Sight
That Black Woman Is Put Together Just Right
Look At Her Black Skin
So Black to The Bone Deep Within
Look At Her Black Chin
Black Grin
She's Black and She's My Black Friend
Black Pretty Toes
Black African Nose
Black African American Clothes
Standing There with That Black African Attitude Pose
Snap A Picture Of Her | It's Captured | Now It's Froze
She Is That
Black
Intact
Black And on Track - Black and Traveling Across My Hearts Map
Black And at The Top of The Stack
So Black and Intelligent and Smart
So Black and Real from The Heart
So Black and In This World Doing Her Part
Black Ain't Wrong
Black Is Beautiful and So Strong
Black Has Been Around for So Long
Black And Stacked Up Like an Ice Cream Cone
She Is That
She's Black and She Has the Black Man's Back
She's Black and She Knows How to Act
She's Black and She's Not on That Ugly Thang Called Crack
She's Black and I Know That

I Love Black - I Am Black
And She Is Black
She Is That
Because That Black Sista Named --------------- Is All That
From Her Head to Her Feet
So Black and Beautiful and Unique
So Black and Sweet
Her Black Attitude Is Just Like a Clean House,
So Tidy And Neat
She Is That
And She, That Beautiful Woman Named ------------ Is Black
As I Turn to Her and Tip My Black Hat

She Is That

I Love You Because

I Love You Because
You Are My Sunshine
I Love You Because
You've Never Clowned Me While I Was Crying
I Love You Because
You Are My Life Raft
I Love You Because
You Make Me Smile and Laugh
I Love You Because
You Are Like the Rain
I Love You Because
You've Taught Me How to Deal With Pain
I Love You Because
You Are Like the Open Sky
I Love You Because
I Know I Wanna Be with You Until The Day I Die
I Love You Because
I Like the Way You Look In My Eye
I Love You Because
You Are Just Like the Water That Flows
I Love You Because
Your Skin Always Smells Like a Rose
I Love You Because
I Love You from Your Head To Your Toes
I Love You Because
I Love the Way You Wear Your Clothes
I Love You Because
You Are Like a Clock, Always On Time
I Love You Because
That's What Made Me Write This Poem with A Rhyme

Grandpa's Little Girl

I can't lie:
She is my entire world.
Such a happy little bundle of joy.
She emerged as a little girl, not a little boy.
My eyes well up with tears.
Hearing her sweet little voice.
She is the primary reason I pray.
For the sun to rise every day.
It means we'll have another whole day to play.
It makes no difference if it's windy, stormy, or sunny. When I hold her little hand, I feel so important it's not funny.
I'm one of the reasons she's on this land.
I want her to grow up properly.
Live an out-of-sight happy and fun life.
I want her to be a respectable woman.
And someone's beautiful wife.. She reminds me of the sun.
It's a lot of fun just talking to her.
I love it when she answers the phone The first thing she says is hello.
I'm not going to lie:
Just hearing that one word makes me want to cry. Then she asks, "Grandpa, what -u- doing?" "Nothing, baby girl," I say.
Gosh, she is my entire world.
I look at her pictures and notice.
How happy her little eyes are.
I had a conversation with God the other day,
He told me,
"Please, son, never tell her lies." So my goal is to teach her.
How to be a loving and caring person.
Being a grandfather is like living in a
fantastic and beautiful dream.
I'm looking at a photo of her.
Barrettes in her hair.
Another image standing on a small chair.

Another was taken on her birthday.
I can't lie;
I'm overjoyed to be here with her today.
I pray to God that we will be able to spend many years together.
I hope He lets us both be as tough as leather.
I wouldn't give her up for anything in the world.
She is Grandpa's granddaughter.
She is my entire world.

P.S. This poem is dedicated to Nhyaree, my granddaughter.
I love her with every breath I take.
She's my ray of sunshine.
She's the person who cheers me up when I'm down. she is the main reason I want my life and
Family to be stable!
I LOVE – U – NHYAREE 4 - EVER

If I Don't Have You

If I don't have you, I think I would lose my mind
I don't even think I'd be able to write poetry with a rhyme
You see, baby you are the page to my life that's been wrote
but never read
You are the only person I see inside my head
That's how I know I'm in love
That's also why I pray day and night
To the higher spirit up above
If I don't have you Then life no longer has a meaning
But as long as I have you, I'll continue dreaming
I see us growing old together
Our humanly bond will be tougher than any leather
And we'll hold hands
And walk thru all types of different weather
We will walk in the rain
You're the picture and I'm the frame
We will walk in the sun
Every day will be happy and fun
We will walk in the snow
And each day, each hour, and year, our relationship will
constantly grow
Because baby you are truly my soulmate and best friend
You are my wife
You are my entire life
If you needed my heart to live,
I'd cut it out of my chest for you with a knife
If I don't have you, I think I would lose my mind
But I do have you, and that's how I'm gonna end this poetry
With a rhyme
I love you with all my heart, so let's both shine
I thought I'd write that poem for you Because you were
heavy on my mind

No Storm Can Last Forever

Look outside at the trippy weather
Raindrops falling to the ground
Listen to the wet sound
There's a storm in our Correctional System
Listen up, while I list "em"
Far too many black men on lock
Brains tied down, like a boat at the dock
Sitting back, watching a motionless clock
Wondering is life alive, like we wonder about Tupac
There are people of all races who can't read or write
Hey C/O please turn on the light
Because tonight this guy is gonna learn how to write
And his mind is gonna fly high into the sky
Just like a kite
In prison there's people who are ill
They are gonna die before they parole, and that's real
As the doctor is steady giving them the wrong pill
Listen to the storm
Listen to the wind blow, it's cold, not warm
There's a ghetto child with no father being born
He came from a drop of sperm and a moment of lust
No storm can last forever, trust
Look at the passion in the cloud
Look in the mirror and tell me
When was the last time you smiled?
Ghetto kids running wild Shooting and killing each other
Last week, a stray bullet killed my homies mother
She's down in her casket listening to the rain
Still trying to get the stray bullet outta her heart that's in pain
She's still trying to preach the word to those lost in the dust,
From cocaine
So numbed up in the brain

Her tears are never getting a chance to dry
As she reaches her hand up in the wet sky
No storm can last forever
Step outside and trip off the trippy weather
But always remember No storm can last forever.

To My Unborn Child

This poem is to my Unborn Child
I can't wait for you step into this world,
that day will make my proud
I want you to scream out I'm here everybody real loud
I hope you inside the womb and the belly getting your thoughts straight
When you come, I'm gonna show you how to love, not hate
I pray that no mishaps happen
I listened to your mama's stomach last night,
and I heard you in there clappin'
You must of heard me reading my poetic words
One day when your old enough I'm gonna talk to you about the Bees and the Birds
Or is it the Birds and the Bees?
I pray that you come out healthy with no disease
Please GOD, I hope you hear me please
I want you to come out sharp as a tack
I want you to learn how to act
I want you to help your mama with the slack
And I want you to respect others It don't matter if they white, Asian, Mexican, or Black
I want you to be color blind
Drugs, I never wanna hear about you buying
I'm telling you the truth, I ain't lying
I want you to study your family tree
I want you to get to know me
We gonna be tight
We'll talk thangs out We should never have to fight
I might not always be right So correct me if I'm wrong
You are my Unborn Child, but I want you to come into this World and be strong
To my Unborn Child
I can't wait for you to come into this world,
And make me proud

To My Born Child

This poem is to my born child
I pray that you don't grow up too wild
I pray that you follow life's rules
Learn all you can in the world's schools
And use your mental tools
Whenever you're hit in the chest with the blues, walk straight
Even if you have a pair of crooked shoes
I want you to learn how to be a gentleman or proper lady
Treat others the way you wanna be treated, not shady
Help others, Respect the worlds mothers
And realize that we're all sisters and Brothers
I want you to seek the real
Express your emotions and outlooks to others
On how you really feel
Protect yourself
Look out for your health
Don't do drugs
Don't sweep your life under negative rugs
Duck and Dodge and realize
In this world there's deadly slugs
There are people who will kill
Act unreal, and not give a damn if your precious blood spills
You have to have safe sex
because if you don't, you'll lay in a casket next
There's people who have no love
That don't believe in the higher spirit up above
I'm gonna teach you about the mistakes I made
I'm gonna teach you how to be sharp as a razor blade
There's a lot going on that you have to be ready for
So think about that when you walk outta that front door
To my Born Child
I hope you hear this poem
I'm kicking at you real loud.

Birth

My poetry and another poem hooked up one day
And they realized that they liked each other in a real way
They went out on dates for coffee and tea, and meals
And one night Ms. Poetry forgot her birth control pills
But my poem Mr. Poetry
Let his words touch and melt her heart
And together they both agreed
To make sweet love in the dark
Their words kissed, a few missed, none dissed
As Mr. Poetry prayed and got his wish
He started to stroke Ms. Poetry all over her poem
Every word, he wanted to understand "em"
So he could flow "em" and know "em"
He put his poem inside hers
And they started to feel the joy
Ms. Poetry got pregnant, and inside her poetry was a boy
He was growing and waiting
Waiting for his chance to experience birth
So that he could step into this poetic earth
So one day Ms. Poetry's water broke
And a young poem was written And it's the one I just spoke
The Birth of Poetry

I Know the Things You've Seen Have Been Cold

But Mama, you have a story that needs to be told
You grew up in the Ghetto
Sometimes I wonder
Have your emotions and feelings ever had a chance to settle
You've seen things I've never seen
You've even had dreams That I've never dreamed
So many didn't come true
So many moments in life that we're sad and blue
As you ran into my daddy Loved him Had sex with him, and
Your stomach grew
First came Alvin, then came me
Ain't that how it went? Don't you agree?
You always took care of us
You loved us and taught us trust
Thank you, Mama, for that because it was a must
You always made sure we had a meal to eat
Clothes on our backs and shoes on our feet
You were faithful to my dad
But I know the things you have seen have been cold and that
Makes me sad
And when daddy used to beat on you,
It would make me mad!
Mama, I swear to God
I wanted to defend you at those times
I wonder if my anger towards dad made me grow up, and
rebel and commit crimes
I wasn't big enough to fight him back
And that's why he used to get away with that
I used to pray at night in my bed
And ask God to make the sun shine inside me and your head
I know the things you've seen have been cold
That's why I'm telling your story because it needs to be told

I remember times
I've looked deep into your face and seen the pain
I commend you Mama because I don't know how the Hell
you made it thru the rain
I wish I could paint all the pictures you've dreamt
I know all you've ever wanted
Was for me and my brother to change
Gosh life is so insane
And some days it's even strange
I remember times I've looked deep into your eyes
And I feel so bad knowing I've told you a lot of lies
But the cold thing about it
I knew that you knew
Because I came from inside of your belly, that means that
I'm a part of you
Why do we think we can lie to our mamas?
I ask myself this question
All these years later I'm still sitting here guessing
I sent you thru so much stress
All these years later, I'm still sorting out all this mess
All these years I've wasted sitting in prisons
All because I didn't listen to you
And made the wrong decisions
I know you never wanted to see me sitting in here
Hey Mama, let me kiss you and wipe away your tears
I haven't been there
We both see it as we sit here and just stare
And take in the air
But Mama, I want you to know I really do care
As I hug you and softly touch your pretty hair
The gray hairs in your head look so youthful
Let me take a minute to be honest and truthful
I know I brought a lot of these gray hairs up out of your
scalp to be seen
I apologize for all the times I might have gotten mad and
was evil and mean
You seen your mom pass, then you seen Artis and Uncle
Johnny go

I know for a while
Life had no meaning no "mo"
But you bounced back real slow
And you started to re-grow
I swear to God, I don't know how you do it
I swear to God I don't know how you got thru it
If it had of been me, I know I would of blew it
Your husband, your soulmate, your best friend
Artis, we all really miss him
Mama, when you cry I cry
At those times I wish we could both just fly
Way up into the beautiful sky
Change this world, and the bad events and times, and see
happiness out of our eye
You've seen family members switch up and act like foes
Look how tight the family is, it really shows I know the
things you've seen have been cold
I give this heartfelt real poem to you Mama in your beautiful
hands to hold
And your painful story has finally been told
I know the things you've seen have been cold

I Got Lots Of Flowers Today

I got a lot of flowers today,
My boyfriend gave them to me
To make up for the fight we had yesterday
I know he really loves me,
That's why I don't trip when he pushes and shoves me,
I know sometimes I make him mad,
And he has to put me in my place,
I'll just put make-up on to cover the bruises and marks on
My beautiful face,
You see my family and friends
Don't realize how much he cares,
And they don't realize how much special time we both share,
He makes the best love to me he makes me feel like
I never have,
He makes me smile and laugh,
I know he's gonna stop beating me.
He's gonna change soon,
He told me this stuff happens in every relationship, up until
the two lovers get in tune,
So I guess you can say we're out of sync,
I got a lot of flowers today, and I don't care what ya'll think,
We went to dinner, shared hugs, and kisses,
And also talked about all of our dreams and wishes,
Check this out,
I woke up this morning and he was quite upset,
His shirt was off and his back was sweaty and wet,
He turned towards me and said,
Have you been fooling around
With that new guy in town?
. I said no, laughed thinking he was playing. He slapped me
hard across the face,

Next thang I know
I was lying on the ground and blood was the taste,
My mouth was busted,
Oh my god this was the man I trusted,
I mean, he never hit me this hard or went this far,
I felt like all of a sudden I was trapped in a little jar,
He kicked me in the head,
Snatched me up and threw me across the bed,
And then started to rape me,
Reshape me,
Duct tape me
I'm thinking to myself this man don't love me,
He must hate me,
But now it's too late
As I watch him unleash his anger and raw hate,
I feel the blows and punches landing,
Now I'm finally understanding,
This is what my family and friends warned me about,
As I frantically look for an escape route,
I'm scared to death in my own house,
being raped and beaten by my own spouse,
Why?
As I start to cry,
As his big fist comes crashing down into my eye,
At this moment, I'm wondering am I about to die.
I see all the flowers he gave me before,
This beating is the worse, I just can't take it anymore,
He grabs something out of his pocket,
Oh my god it's some brass knuckles,
He looks at me and starts to chuckle
He places them on his hands,
And follows through with his evil plans,
After the 4th blow I didn't remember nothing,
My heart stopped real sudden,
I died of shock and trauma,

The last thang I pictured was my mama,
I'm looking down at myself lying in my casket,
I'm really gone gosh, life is so drastic,
My face doesn't even look real, my face it looks plastic
It's strange that I got a lot of flowers today,
But I can no longer enjoy them in a special kind of way,
I can't smell "em"
Or touch "em"
Or even put "em" in a vase.
(Wake up ladies getting beat on)
And please look at my beat-up face,
I got a lot of flowers today,
And they are on top of my casket in a real tragic way,
I got a lot of flowers today..

Aborted

Think how many lost out on their chance to walk this earth.
The reason why is because they were aborted at birth.
Never even got a chance to step a foot on this earth.
To see what life is really worth.
I wonder if they had of been born who
would they had of been?
Would they had of sinned?
Would they had of ended up being my kin?
I wonder if they would of been my real friend?
I think as I sit here, how they screamed
When the doctor killed them.
Man, they thought this doctor was
Supposed to be the one to be real to them.
Yet instead, he was ill to them.
Who are we to say that they can no longer breathe?
Who are we to say that they can't stay, they gotta leave?
Did you wanna be aborted?
Screaming to live in the world but in pain face contorted.
I'm so mad that I can't even see straight.
I think every little baby should be born and have a chance to stand at home plate.
Let him or her take their swings.
Let him or her have their chance to share dreams.
Do you world really hear my poetic screams?
This world is so wrong,
always screaming to those in pain to stay strong.
This world thinks that it's so right.
Always aborting another child
It's going on right now as I write
And I'm truly uptight.
Look at that fetus study that little fetus.
Hold & touch that little fetus.

How the hell world can you mistreat us?
Where do our souls go when we get done this way?
Do they just run astray?
Do they get with the other Aborted kids
And go outside and play?
What if it was you?
What would you do?
They never even got a chance to share
With us thoughts from their brain.
They never got to even see the rain.
They never even got a chance to reach fame.
All they ever experienced was aborted pain.
I feel like I'm going insane.
Wouldn't it be a trip if they could rewind you
Like a cassette tape.
Back into a baby or fetus getting ready to abort you,
Wouldn't you be in bad shape?
Look at the whole aborted cake.
It has all flavors in it, what piece do you wanna take?
The black one?
The white one?
Or the brown one?
Think about it as you read this poem
And enjoy the rays from the sun.
Abortion isn't even fun.
That aborted baby never got to see the sun.
Never got a chance to walk or run.
Never got a chance to even have fun.
I could of adopted them and made them my daughter or son.
Right now I'm so exhausted.
My thoughts & brain are so frosted.
I heard about another abortion last night.
I almost lost it.
This poem I just wanna take it and toss it.

Let it just fly in the air like a kite. Because all of us know
abortion ain't right.
Gosh life is so - so cold.
Each & every day I look in the mirror I'm starting to get old.
But that aborted fetus doesn't even get this chance, and this
story needs to be told.
Wrap this poem in a warm blanket like a baby.
Read it world, and don't you say maybe.
Maybe you're right, maybe you're wrong?
You know you feel me deep down inside to your bones.
Think how many lost out on their chance to walk this earth.
The reason why, is because they were aborted at birth.
Never even got a chance to step foot on this earth.
And they never even got the chance to see
what a life is really worth.
Because they were aborted at birth.

It's a Baby -N- Her Tummy

Growing each day and each time the clock ticks
She's wondering how she let herself get caught up
-N-
This pregnancy Mix
She met a cute dude
Loved his saucy attitude
But once he got her pregnant, he became hella rude

When they first met, he took her everywhere he went
When he asked her for sex, she thought his love for her was solid as cement
He bought her all kinda of gifts and stuff
But now she's pregnant and by herself now life is ruff

It's a Baby -N- Her Tummy
The other day at school all the girls called her a big dummy
She felt so used and abused
That she blew a fuse
She for her father's gun
Hunted down her soon-to-be Baby's Daddy
Ex-Boyfriend
Who was on the run
She caught him in his neighborhood hugging another girl
Laughing and having fun
Her whole mission was to shoot and kill him and take his life from under the sun
She did just that
Shot him 3 times right through his hat
He's laid out flat
His unborn child is kickin' inside her stomach real hard
As a vision flashed to her mind of doing life on a prison yard
So, she raises the gun to her head

Fills it with lead
And now her, her unborn baby, and dude are dead
Such a dad story, ending with no glory
Message to ya'll young girls getting knocked up
Close your legs and keep "em" locked up
And don't let it be a Baby -n- your Tummy
Because it's up to you to be Smart or a Dummy

Suicide

She Was So Young and Lost
She Couldn't See Thru Life's Suicide Frost
Suicide Sat Just Like Frosting on a Cake
Suicide is Why Her Young Body is Dead,
That's Real Not Fake
She Tried Pills
They Took Her on Cheap Thrills
Had Her Thoughts Switching Reels
Had Her Different Personalities Stumbling Up Hills
She Tried Cutting Her Wrists
But The Main Vein and Artery | She Missed
She Still Didn't Pay Attention to Gods Life Filled Kiss
She Stayed Trapped Inside of Satan's Death Wish
So, She Decided to Step in Front of a Moving Car
She Got 25 Broken Bones Star
And Laid in The Hospital for Almost a Year by Far
She Got Back Strong and Healthy but Her Mind Was Still Broken
Believe Me, I'm Not Jokin'
Satan Was Still Tappin' Each Day on Her Shoulder
And This Is What He Told Her
"You Young Lady Will Die for Me Today
And I Promise
You Will Die from Suicide If You Do It This Way
Jump Off That 150-Foot Bridge
And Tonight, You Will Lay at The Morgue in A Fridge
So, She Jumped and Took Her Young Life
I Don't Understand Why She Didn't Get Help for Her Strife
Or For Her Pain
Suicide It Was the Blame
In Remembrance of Those Lost.

Rape

Rape
Mind And Body | Gaped
Feelings, Emotions, And Outlooks Towards Men,
Bent Outta Shape
None Of This Can Be Put Back Together with Tape
Picture The Scene
Picture What I Mean
Rape It Isn't a Dream
As I Hurt Deep Within,
As I Watch That Raped Woman Scream
He Snatched Her, Scratched Her
Then He Attacked Her
He Let a Moment of Lust
Eliminate His Trust
As He Screams at Her, And Tells Her to Hush
The Place Is Inside Her Own Bedroom
She Felt Like She Was Up on The Moon
You See He Snuck into Her House While She Was Out
He Already Knew What He Was Gonna Do | No Doubt
She Walked In | He Hit Her on The Chin
At That Moment She Wondered
Was Life for Her Gonna End
So, She Started to Fight Back from Deep Within
What Was Happening to Her | She Knew Was a Sin
As He Ripped Her Clothes Off and Forced Himself In
Inside Her Womanhood
All He Was Thinking Was This Feels Good
While She Was Thinking of a Way to Kill This Crazy
Stranger If She Could
All She Felt Was Raw Pain
A Sense of Unexplainable Shame
From Her Eyes Jumped Out Drops | Of Salty Rain

She Knew Life Would Never Be the Same
Who Could She Blame?
As She Screamed Out God's Name
Oh God Help Me Please
Sick Folks Raping Like This Is a Serious Disease
As Her Legs, And Her Muscles | She Tried to Squeeze
She Swung Back - Scratched His Face, Arms and Back
As He Hit Her in The Head and Her Whole World Went
Completely Black
Black As Night
Her Body No Longer Could Fight
This Poem Right Here I Had to Write
Because Rape It Just Ain't Right
I Hear the Guy | Grunting and Groaning
Truth Is They Need to Catch Him
And Line Him Up for A Stoning
Death By Stoning
Reason Is for This Unlawful Boning
As The Woman Wakes Up from This Abuse
Still Trying to Find a Way to Get Loose
Trying To Figure Out a Way to Save Her Life
And Reach with This Animal/A Truce
Inside Her Head She Is Having Crazy Thoughts
Some Of Them Are Bunched Up in Knots
Thrown In the Corner Like Dirty Socks
All He's Concerned About Is Disrespecting Her Flesh
Like An Animal Tearing Meat/Off Some Ham Hocks
She Really Starts to Use Her Mind
Sucks It Up and Stops Crying
She Remembers Underneath Her Pillow She Has a Knife
All She's Thinking About Is Taking This Animals Life
Her Hand Slides Across Her Sheets Real Smooth
She Knows She Has to Make All the Right Moves
With Her Other Hand She Touches His Back & Arm
As She Looks Thru Tears in Her

Eyes and Knows in Her Heart
She's Gonna Fight Thru This Storm
He Says You Like What I'm Doing to You?
As He Throws Her Legs Up in The Air
Starts To Grab Her Hair
All Of a Sudden, He Feels an Impact Like the Punch of a Grizzly Bear
It's The Knife Going in And Out
Out And In
As A Vision Flashes Inside His Head
That His Life Is About to End
For His Deceitful Sin
Her Anger Is So Strong
Down To the Bone
As He Rolls Off of Her and Bumps into The Nightstand | And the Phone
She Tells Him You Shouldn't Have Raped Me
Because I'm A Woman | And I Live All Alone
She Calls the Police and Before You Know it, They Are There
As She Sits in A Chair
Staring At Empty Air
Wondering Why Life Is So Uneven and Unfair
The Officer Tells Her That the Animal Is Dead
She Never Heard a Word That He Said
She Has Blocked Out the World Instead
I Feel Her Pain
I Know She Feels Like Going Insane
But Me the Poet, I Step in The Room and Have a Quiet Seat Inside Her Brain
And Tell Her Young Lady, I Know You Feel Like You've Been Hit by A Train
But It's Not Your Fault - So Don't Feel Ashamed
Take Some Time to Heal -To Chill - To Once Again Feel
Because You Woman Are Deeply Real

When You Feel You're Back | Let Us Know
Because We Love You, And Want You to Continue to Grow
Because Being Raped Is a Devastating Blow

Dedicated To the Women Who Have Been Raped!!!

Chapter Four – Redemption
This Letter Is Dedicated to Those Who Have Died Over Nothing, and to Those Spending Life in Prison Over Nothing!

Over Nothing!!

This is not going to be a story about a sinner finding God in prison. This is not a story about a sinner reaching to you or telling you to change, this letter is a wake-up call to all those who are blind to reality. I'm just like you, I'm a sinner. We all are, there's no one perfect in this world, the only one that was, came and died for our sins so that we may have chance.

Now I know that most you have been taught and told that only the strong survive? That is partly true, and I agree that we must protect ourselves and our families at all costs. However, protecting a street corner, a park, or a hood, is not worth spending the rest of your life in prison. I'm sure that if you had a chance to ask a homie, or relative who has been killed in the deadly game of gangbanging, he or she would tell you that nothing was accomplished or gained, so their death was in vain.

You still don't own that street or park or barrio, set, hood or etc. It belongs to the city you live in. All you did was do this job the police are paid to do, "serve and protect." All in all, they died for someone else's property. We go into a rage due to the loss of a homie or relative and it causes us to seek revenge or retaliation. Someone else is killed or hurt, yeah it feels good for a minute to get them back, until you're in prison for the rest of your life over nothing, over your stupidity. Guess what? Now two people are dead, you still don't own that street, park, or hood, and you're in prison for life. Which means you can't take care of your family, you lost everything you had.

Most likely, you will see (3) thangs for the first time. First, you see that the same people you were going to war against now stand together with you, because of your race. The second thing you will see is a complete stranger who calls shots for your people, telling you to leave your hatred and animosity for that hood, barrio or set on the streets. Yes, the streets you'll never see again. Now the third thing you will see is that the only people by your side are your mother and perhaps some family, but usually it's your mother. You lost your wife or girlfriend, and the homies don't have no time for you anymore. They're on the streets having fun, getting high, partying, etc., but not you. You're stuck in prison over nothing, and guess what you will learn while you are spending your life in prison? The hardest part of doing time is when your mother - father, brother, sister, or child dies and you are not allowed to go to the funeral and pay your respects. Or worse, someone kills one of your family members over something you caused, and you can't do nothing!

Perhaps you may be thinking that it can't happen to you because it happened to me. It was all fun and games until someone died, and I was charged with murder, and sent to prison for the rest of my life. It didn't have to happen, if only I would have learned by the mistakes of the other people that went thru the same thing! Does this story seem like fun? Perhaps it seems scary? No, it's neither one, it's the truth of where your life is heading if you are gangbanging. There are so many guys here just like me doing life for nothing.

You Can ask any one of us if it was stupid and not worth it? Doing life in prison and nothing getting accomplished or gained is a stupid way to choose to go in life. The scary part is never getting out and dying in prison over nothing. Every day I wake up and say to myself, "I lost it all over nothing." Every night I beg the lord to forgive me of my sins and have mercy on me and give me another chance at freedom. I promise God I will never do it again. I ask him to please give me a chance. He did give us all a chance when he sent his only son to die for our sins.

If you out there or inside, please wake up to reality and realize that there's no future in gangbanging. Stop the killing and hurting of God's children. We all need to understand that life is too short to be wasted in prison over nothing. Jesus is lord and he's coming soon for his homies. Are you one of them? Get right or get left behind. God bless -you all, and remember, it can happen to you.

OVER NOTHING!

When Will I Smile Again?

Such a cold question just hanging in the air.
If I smile again, I wonder who will really care.
My facial muscles just don't work to form a smile,
But they did when I was a young child.
I smiled all the time,
But lately as an adult, all I do is a bunch of crying.
How can you smile when your generation is dying?
Giving up on this beautiful thang called life,
No longer trying.
Smile at that,
Then tell me, was your smile fake or real black?
How can you smile when your mama is strung out on crack?
Please tell me because seeing this going on in this world has
My mind off track.
My thoughts are like a derailed train,
Flipped upside down, shattered feeling pain.
I'll be able to smile again if I can crush every cocaine pipe.
Turn on inside of the entire World's head,
A bright beautiful light,
I wonder how can you smile
When your entire race is sitting around behind bars?
Never getting a fair chance
To reach and touch the world's stars,
Just lost and outta touch sittin' in a 8X10 cell,
Never living well, going through hell,
Falling apart as they began to yell
Such a Cold story to tell.
When will I smile again?
I think about this every day,
As I run my black hand across my chin.
When will I smile again?

Sittin' -N- A Cage!!

Just Sittin' -n- a Cage
Wings Clipped So I Can't Fly,
Mind In a Cold Rage.
I Wanna Fly Like I Did When I Was Little
Sittin' -n- a Cage
Gosh, Life Is Like a Difficult Riddle.
My Wings Used to Spread for Miles Across The Earth
Now That My Wings Have Been Clipped,
I See What Freedom Is Really Worth.
Let Me Fly, Fly High. Fly Up Into The Sky.
Give Me My Wings Back,
So I Can Try.
I Just Wanna Take Off Running,
Like I've Lost My Mind.
Just Sittin' -n- a Cage
I See a World Full Of Wingless Folks Dying
Without My Wings Has Me Crying
I Cry, I Cry High, I Cry Up Into The Sky
I See a Pair Of Wings In My Eyes
Waving At Me Goodbye
I'm Just Sittin' -n- This Cage
I'm Like an Incomplete Book That's Missing A Page
Wings Clipped So I Can't Fly
Mind In A Cold Rage
Just Let Me Fly, Fly High, Fly Up Into The Sky
Give Me Back My Wings
So I Can Try.
Sittin' -n- a Cage

A Poem Asking the System To Give Me Back My Wings.

My Generation!

My Generation is out of control,
Before 21- know it, everybody is going be on parole.
A whole generation looking at the world from behind bars,
Never getting' a fair chance at reaching' for the stars.
It's really a sad sight,
But I need all the help I can get, to make it right.
My Generation.
It's a lot of coldness that we are facing,
As I write, I begin pacing, My thoughts are racing.
I hear the gunfire,
I really wonder when my generation is gonna expire.
Because we're all walking on a thin piece of wire,
Bald-head, empty thoughts just like a well-worn tire.
My Generation.
Is out of control,
And today it's seriously taking a toll.
School Shootings,
Classrooms sprayed with students' blood.
Books not being read,
As another Gang-member gets killed today over the colors
Blue & Red.
Is my Generation really dying?
No longer trying,
Should I stop all this crazy crying?
Yes, I'm crying for change,
My Generation is acting deranged.
My Generation.
Do they really care?
As I sit here, and into space, I just stare.
What is making them not want to do right?
It seems they enjoy violence and the ugly word called fight.
Why is everybody so uptight?
Smack-N-The Middle,
My Generation is just like a difficult riddle.
I find it difficult at times

To get the subject squarely-N-my sights,
I hope God can help me reach
My Generation
With m poetry turn on some lights.
My Generation…!!!

I'm Just Dropping' Lyrics from The Top of My Head
Big Words That You Can Understand

Step back and look at the true essence of yourself my man
Really read this poem sitting in your hand
Conventional, Commonplace
Let me put, like make-up, my conversation
And poetry on your face
Make my thoughts and ink pen convulse
'Which means violently shake
Step back, big words are about to break
Counterbalance, weight that balances another
Why are those lost souls that gang bang not using their talents, Hurting their mother
Controversy, Crescendo Inn-u-win-doe
Crack cocaine has you slim though
Distraught were those the thangs you were taught
Urban Abyss words, tied up in a knot
Cascade, thru murky water we wade
In life, some people got it made
Millionaires chilling in the shade
Controversial, Complicated
Urban Abyss poetry
I wonder has it finally made it?
Ain't nuttin' big about these words
The title of this poem
It flew into my head and mind like a flock of birds
Who is the poet?
That flow it
That blow it
That know it

Take it and show it
Look and study the picture inside the picture
Inside of that picture is another picture
Waiting to be placed right next to another picture
You get the picture?
I promise you'll be able to see the picture
Hey, I gotta head back home to the ghetto
I got some poetry over there warming up in the kettle
Waiting to get its chance to settle
Big words that you can understand
Really read this poem sitting in your hand

Talking Inside My Casket

Damn I'm dead | for real | thangs are drastic
Feet - face body and hands look plastic
Let me hold a conversation with you about my death
Let me express to you how bad I want back my breath
(7) shots - (7) bullets hitting the spot
Life for me stopped on the world's clock
I died due to hanging out in the set
Look at mama's eyes soaking wet
Ring the tears out like you would a dish rag
I'm inside my casket | pants pulled up I no longer pulled
Down with a sag
No longer inside my pocket is a blue-green - black - grey - brown - or red rag
Somebody, turn on the light down here
Please turn it on - so I can see clear
Damn you couldn't have told me last year - I'd die this year
I'm inside my casket and I can't even sip a soda or beer
I can't go to my folk's pop warner games
And any longer cheer
I can't even hear my mama's familiar voice calling my name all up in my ear
I can't walk down the street
I can't look down at a pretty pair of tennis shoes on my feet
I can't even say I'm going to do this or that next week
I'm down inside my casket wishing - and dreaming
Wanting my shot at life again I look at me screaming
Then I saw a bright light
My body shook and put up a weak fight
And then I flew to a distant place like a lite kite
When I got there | this dude was reading and writing poetry
He was real good
I looked deep into his face
And realized he was my old friend from my hood

He said you made it here just like me before your time
We both hugged | and started crying
He said some force is gonna
Come and take your human shell
and then another force is gonna come and determine if
you're going to heaven or hell
But inside your casket is where your person and flesh
I will always dwell
No more kicking it at the pad watching T.V.
No more wearing pretty expensive jewelry
No more eating food
No more acting tuff showing off your attitude
It's all over dude
Think real hard about
if you really wanna die because when you do
You'll be inside your casket talking
like me and it ain't even fly
As I open my casket just enough
to throw this poem up into the sky
Talking inside my casket
Death is real it's not plastic
Thangs are drastic

It's Happening Too Often

It's happening too often
Another one of my homies lying in a coffin
Oh believe it, he's really dead
(4) bullets to the body and (4) bullets to the head
Study the pain in my boy's face
Black-on-Black gang violence, such a waste
I'll never enjoy it, spit it out such a bad taste
I wonder what my boy is doing six feet down under the earth
I wonder is he thinking about a chance to have re-birth
I wonder if he finally
Appreciating what his life was really worth
He died representing his hood, he called it his turf
Tears are talking to my eyes
Telling my eyes that they wanna come out and cry
I let "em" fall, until they decide to dry
As I look up and see GOD
And all my homies talking up in the sky
I see my homies mamas living in pain
I see my homies mamas walking slowly thru the rain
I see my homies blood swirling down that ghetto sewer drain
I'm wondering when the sunshine is gonna come
And once again shine on their brain,
And take away this ugly rain
They just put my boy in his grave yesterday
I'm sitting here thinking about him in a real way
Who really cares
As us ghetto soldiers sit tight here on these broken stairs,
grouped up into pairs
I wanna cry again, but instead I laugh
But then the pain is too deep,
So the tears give my eyes another bath

As I add up the dead homies and try to understand this
senseless gang violence math
I start laughing, crying, screaming, dreaming, and shaking.
I'm going insane, I ain't faking
Each killing, my head is breaking
I hear my boy talking to me
From his grave down in his coffin
He's telling me this killing each other, is happening too often
He told me, dog I was just alive (5) days ago
What happened dog? I really wanna know
All-I could do was drop-his obituary on the flo,
And rest my body, brain, and head against my bedroom doe
Is it safe for me to walk outside?
Will the color of my outfit and clothes disrespect and upset
some gang members pride?
To tell you the GOD to honest truth, I'm scared inside
My boy left his little son behind crying
He yelled to me last night from his grave
Dog I'm tired of all of us dying
I felt it in his voice, my boy wasn't lying
He told me to tell his baby's mama
That he was very sorry for sending her thru so much drama
He also told me to take care of his beautiful mama
He was just trying to grow up and be a man
But first he had to get all the childish sides out of himself,
That was his game plan
He said it's finally peaceful,
But damn down here it's really dark
He said, this ain't where I'm supposed to be
I'm supposed to be with my family doing my part
As he reaches his hand outta his coffin,
And touches his mama's broken heart
He said if I could live my life any different
I'd ask GOD to give me back my precious breath
And then we wouldn't be all sad over my unexpected death

My homie opened his coffin
and shook my hand and said good-bye
We both cried for a few minutes
And wiped the tears from our eyes
I handed him some pictures of all those he once knew
I told him I'm gonna do all I can to get my race to stop
killing over the colors red and blue
My homie laid back down and closed his coffin
And my last words were
IT'S HAPPENING TOO OFTEN..

I Look in
My Young Homies Eyes

And I wonder does he see what I see?
A twisted society
And prison system doing us in don't you agree?
They don't give a damn about us
But. They got the nerve to tell us to trust
I can't young homie - I feel if I do - my heart will bust
Inside my young homies eyes - 1 see fear – I see a tear
I see pain - I see shame
I see a young black youth reaching for fame
I see anger - sometimes I see a stranger
I see his life hanging like an old shirt on a hanger
I see danger
I see love
I see someone wanting a hug
I see a young cat trying to make it
But he's forced to sell an ugly drug
I see him ducking and dodging a big slugg
I see poetry floating inside his young mugg
I see the ghetto so clear
I see another life taken sitting
At the bottom of a ice-cold beer
I see him crying I see him really trying
As I sit here and into his eyes I'm prying
I see inside of my young homies eyes
A person who wants to live
Who wants to give
Who wants to breathe
Who wants to achieve
who wants to no longer grieve
I see inside of my young homies eyes an open casket
I see him tearing out of a bag of plastic

Trying to step into this big world and make people see
That all he wants is to be black-intelligent and free
I look inside my young homie's eyes

Urban Ghetto Living

Mama in the kitchen cooking
My sisters and brothers are standing there looking
Listening to the bacon sizzle
Urban ghetto living, chip at it with a chisel
I smell the buttered down toast
I see the ruff black pain filled faces up and down the coast
I can't lie I love these people the most
These people are just like me
Urban ghetto living chained down searching to be free
I hear the plates clacking and rattling together a
Outside it's sunny and hot
They call it beautiful weather
But for some reason, I just see it as another day
Another day to go outside and just play
We even used to play in the rain
Really what we were doing
Was trying to wash away the pain
The pain of knowing that one of our loved ones was strung
out on crack cocaine
I Smell the crack smoke mixed with my eggs yolk
Cold words I just spoke
But I can't lie, my heart is broke
Mama is putting the silverware on top of the table
Urban ghetto living is real, It's not a fable
You can't cut it off and on just like watching cable
Turn the pages in the urban abyss books
Why is it a world full of our black youth turning into crooks?
Stop don't turn another page
Really study life and why it's going on in this stage
Mama's pulling down the cups, pouring the milk
Grandma's sitting in her wheelchair,

Hidden halfway under a quilt
No it's not made outta silk
Times is hard, but we gonna make it
I'm looking around, shit I can't fake it
All we can do is just take it
Poke our chest out and stand tall
Brace ourselves for the next time we have to fall
And just pray to god, as we lean our backs against the wall
Bacon, toast, and eggs
Urban ghetto living is standing on two strong legs
Stand up with me and vent some positive rage
Now sit back down and let's pray and eat
Ain't Mama's food good, damn it's so sweet
Seasoned just right
I pictured this Sunday morning breakfast as I laid in my bed last night
Bullets flying, my young friends dying
Our urban ghetto living mama's hearts shattered and crying
I see the clothes that we all wore and passed down, hanging on the clothesline
People in high places
I know you see us trying
I know you feel we can do more
But first you gotta open back up that closed door
So I can soar
Soar up into the Ghetto sky Because up there at the top
Is our piece of pie It's not a lot,
But we'll learn one day how to share
Urban ghetto living, I smell it so strong up in the air
Whew, Mama's meal was all so good
But I'll end this poem by saying
I'm doing all I can to get up outta the hood

Gone With the Wind!

One Minute I'm Here,
Crawling, Walking, Then Running
The Next I'm Gone with The Wind
I See Myself Strolling Down a Long Unlit Road,
Wondering Has My Soul Been Sold,
Gosh! The Wind Is So Cold.
Flashes Of Childhood Days.
Teenage Unexplainable Ways,
My Adult Life Has Been a Big Crazy Maze.
We Come into This World,
We See It, We Touch It, We Make an Impact In It.
But Don't Ever 4-Get God Began It.
I Reach Out to Touch and Nothing is There.
Just Empty Air,
As I Sit Here in This Poetic Chair,
And Just Look at This Air with An Empty Stare!
It's Strange There Comes a Day When We Must Go.
And When We Go,
We'll Be Gone with The Wind

From The Top of Rooftops!

I Look at The World From The Tops Of Rooftops
And The Thangs I See Makes My Heart Drop
Nobodies Listening, Nobodies Any Longer Caring
Tempers Worldwide Are Flaring
As I Sit on This Rooftop Just Staring
It's So Hard to Laugh
The Whole World Needs a Good Bath
And Then Everyone Needs to Be Placed on A Positive Path
Hold-Up Let Me Add Up the Math
It's So Easy to Cry
Look Close into My Face and Study the Mathematic
Problems In My Eye
Add'em, Subtract'em, Divide'em,
Now Slide'em, Provide'em
Now Bring'em Back Together and Unite'em
Erase The Crack-Erase the Heroin & Meth
I Wanna Breathe & Exhale A Deep Healthy Breath
Erase The Guns
I'm Tired of Them Killing Our Daughters and Sons
Bury The Bullets and Take the Fingers Off the Triggers
Please World Quit Calling Us Black Niggers
Learn With Me, Study with Me, Teach Me, Reach Me
Hold An Intelligent Human Speech with Me
Pour Bleach on Everything That Is Evil and Dirty
And Not Clean
Don't Lock Him Up Please Help the Dope Fiend
T
The Judge & The D.A Many Have Gotten High
You Won't Believe It Because
You Can't See the Truth in Your Eye!
It Happens, It Goes On

They Did It Because the Drugs Was Too Strong
I Look at The World from The Tops of Rooftops
And The Thangs I See Makes My Heart Drop
Body Parts Being Sold
People Being Struck Out for Nothing,
Life Ending in A Cold Cell
Such A Sad Story Being Told
Babies Dying, Nobodies Even Crying
Remember God See's You, He's Up in Heaven Spying
Spying On You
You Better Watch the Thangs That You Do
That Goes for Ya'll That Are Killing
Over the Colors Red And Blue,
I Look at The World from The Tops Of Rooftops
And The Thangs I See Makes My Heart Drop.

The Ghetto

The Ghetto streets seem to have taken on a life of their own.
I noticed that last night as I stood here all alone.
The sidewalk has turned into a wild beast.
That's the way they looked to me
when I walked thru my hood,
In Southeast.
The telephone poles turned into angry giants.
So Defiant
The stop signs were imaginary fake soldiers
Posted all the time.
Wherever us Ghetto kids died at, those signs stood crying.
I'm telling you the truth homie, I ain't lying!
The houses turned into hollow spaces.
Just sitting there every day studying our Ghetto faces.
Never even thinking about switching places.
Never even worrying about catching cases
The cars lined up on the streets
Were always frozen in formation.
Chilling like they were on a cheap vacation.
The Ghetto Schools,
They were the place a lot of us broke rules.
Thought we were sharpening our tools.
All we were concerned about
Was who had on the tightest shoes.
Nothing added up in the ghetto.
It was always tossed up, never getting a chance to settle.
I wonder does heaven really have a ghetto?
Angry Ghetto kids releasing frustration
On each other like hot tea kettles
There was constant death,
Lost souls stealing each other's precious breath.

I look back into the ghetto, now there's nothing left.
I feel like right now that…
The Ghetto is zipped up like a pair of pants,
As I unzip "em" and look inside and take a quick glance.
The Ghetto has a lot of patches of dirt.
The Ghetto has a lot of people
Inside of it wallowing around hurt.
The Ghetto has a lot of people
Inside of it that can't even afford a shirt.
I see the Ghetto streetlight beaming
I see a Ghetto youth chasing a drop of precious semen
Hoping he can save another Ghetto life for real
Instead of Dreaming
The Ghetto streets seem to have taken on a life of their own
I noticed this last night as I stood Here All Alone.

Free At Last!

Free at last, free at last!
It's time to take my broken poetry up out of this cast.
It's no longer broken.
It's my way of being soft-spoken.
Let it run thru your veins.
Let it mix in with your blood.
Let it stick in your mind
Like a pair of shoes stuck -n- mud.
My poetry is free at last!
Read all of it and have a blast.
I got messages for everybody walking.
After they read my poetry,
They'll be calling each other & talking.
Martin Luther King Jr. said, "I'm free at last!"
Lord I'm free at last!
It's time to take my broken poetry up out of this cast.
My poetry always seemed to hurt itself.
That's why all these years it's been sitting up on a shelf.
But now it's free at last!
Because five minutes ago
The poetry doctor released it out of this cast.

FREE AT LAST, FREE AT LAST

Wake Up And Stop The Genocide

Wake Up And Stop The Genocide
Please I'm Begging My Race -2- Stop the Genocide-
Man For Real I'm Hurting Deep Inside-
It's All the Way to The Core
Black On Black Violence/With My Own Race
I'm At War-
I'm Ready -2- Kill Another Black Man with Ease
We Have the Same Color Skin Bro/Stop the Genocide
What Is the Solution -2- This Wicked Disease-
You Ask Me Do I Have All the Answers to Fix
What's Broken-?
Look At All the Real Homies Here with Me We
Are All Trying -2- Stop the Genocide/I'm Not Joking-
My Beautiful Black Race My Words Are Well Spoken-
Let's Sit Down Face -2- Face and Have a Quiet Little Talk
Look At All of Us Killed By Each Other/Lets Take
A Quiet Little Walk-
Don't Be Afraid to Look but Isn't That Your
Little Brother/Outlined with Homicide Chalk-
Crip & Blood
Man That Big Bullet Is Color Blind, Yes I'm
Talking About That Deadly Slugg-
It Doesn't Care About the Colors
Blue Or Red-
All It Cares About Is That You're
Really Dead-
You Better Look at That Picture Real Close-
I'm Your Closest Homeboy/But I Killed You And
Set -U- Up/But I Always Told You That You Could
Trust Me and That I Love You the Most-
Am I Real or Fake? -
Ain't That Crazy How I Was Crying and Falling

All Over Your Casket at Your Wake-
I'm The One Who Put You in the 14kt Gold Casket-
Death And Genocide Is Real Neither One
It's Plastic-
Us Killing One and Other Its Getting Really
Drastic-
I Reach Out to Shake Your Strong Black Hand-
Tell Me Something My Black Race/Genocide
Who Came Up with This Evil Plan-
We Hated by Some Whites and Also Folks
In Other Races-
We Are Packed Inside These Wicked Jails & Prisons
Behind Trumped Up Cases-
Go Through All the Millions/Of Mug Shots And
Look At All of Our Black Stressed Out Faces-
After We Kill Each Other /Our Mothers Are
Left To Deal with All the Pain-
Look At All of Our Mothers on Their Knees
At The Gravesites/Did I Paint a Real Picture and Leave
It Inside Your Brain
This Genocide It Can't Be Washed Away With
<u>God's</u> Beautiful Rain-
Look At Me Laying Dead in The <u>Set</u> on The Street
I Always Hung Out <u>At</u>
Tell Me Something, Why Do We Hate Each Other
I'm Talking to Everybody That God Created
Whites, Asians, Mexicans & Blacks-
I Reach Out to Touch Your Heart but There's
Nothing There-
Wake Up and Stop the Genocide, Damn Bro
I Really Do Care-
As I Sit Inside My Casket Running My Fingers
Through My Hair-
You Stole My Chance to Be Somebody Here On
This Earth
Listen Bro, We Only Get One Chance at This
Thang Called Birth-
I Can't Go Back Inside of My Mama's Body

And Be Born Again-
Damn Black Man, This Genocide Bullshit
Has Got to Come -2- An End-
We Have Lost Too Many Homies To This
Gang Banging-
To This Dope Slanging-
And -2- This "Genocide Don't You Hear
The Phone Ranging-
It's Another One Gone-
Tell Me Something Homies When We
Gon Get Strong-
Let's Pull 2-Gether/Our Entire Race
Let's Be Real With Each Other/Are Me
And You Supposed to Be in That Little Vase-
That's My Ashes/That's All My Family Has Left-
Man I Wish This Poem Could Give Back to All
My Fallen Genocide Soldiers/Back Their Precious Breath-
Breathe Again-
Get Up Out of That Casket and Never
Leave Again-
I'm Tired of All the Killings and The Gunfire-
I'm Tired of The Corrupt System And
Higher Ups Calling Us a Liar-
Man Open Your Eyes, It's <u>Us</u> Killing <u>Us</u>-
Damn Just Last Year It Was Thousands That
Us Blacks Killed on The Ghetto Streets
Man My Heart Is About -2- Bust
Man We Ain't Even Doing Our Homework We
Probably Killing Someone in Our Bloodline
We Need -2- Really Check the Leaves On
Our Family Trees, I Ain't Lying-
Let's Wake Up and Stop the Genocide
-4 Real-
Let's Stop Treating Each Other So Ill-
I Got the Medication, It's in That Bottle
It's Just One Little Pill-
All You Gotta Do Is Swallow It and Let It Get Into
Your Bloodstream-

And Let's Do Like Martin Luther King Jr. Said
Let's All Have a Dream-
Put Your Dream 2-Gether with Mines-
And I Promise on Jesus We'll Be Fine-
You Wear Your Colors, I'll Wear Mines Without
Looking Over Our Shoulder-
Let's Put Down the Guns and Watch How We'll
Start To Grow Older-
Let's Teach This Generation How -2- Be Gladiators
In The Right Way-
Let's Watch Our Race Grow and Multiple Today
Please Wake Up and Stop the Genocide-
Damn Bro, I'm Hurting Deep Down Inside-
Are You Really Resting in Peace?
Man, This Crazy Genocide Has Got -2- Cease
Man, Homie I Miss Seeing You Strolling
Thru The Streets of Southeast-
Let The Pain and The Anger, Let It Go-
Let's Let Our Brains and Our Hearts
Just Grow-
Let's Let Our Love -4- Each Other Flow-
What Are We Fighting -4-/Look at Us Mean
Mugging Each Other Standing Toe-2-Toe-
Man We Got the Same Paint Job From God
He Spray Painted Us <u>Black</u> Man, You My Bro
I Shouldn't Have-2-Be Afraid of My
Own Kind-
I Shouldn't Have to Talk About Us Killing
Each Other In Poetry with A Rhyme-
I Shouldn't Have to Keep Sitting Here
Losing My Mind
If We Make Up and Stop the Genocide
I Promise You Will Be Fine-
Look Me in My Eyes Brother I Ain't Lying-
For Us to Stop Killing Each Other Ain't
Gonna Make Us Soft and Weak-
I'm Going to Sit My Rag/My Gun/ And My
Attitude Down on The Ground, Walk Away

From It All, Thank You for Letting Me Speak-
Let's Wake Up and Stop the Genocide-
For The Last Time I'm Telling You
I'm Hurting Deep Down Inside -
All The Way to The Core-
Black On Black Violence/With My Own Race
I'm At War-

Written By Aaron Lamar Bryant
A.K.A. The Poet
Dn 7-31-22
At 9:30 Am

This Poem Is Dedicated to Every Black Man in The World That Has Died at The Hands of Another Black Man, I Wish I Could Bring All Ya'll Back! And It's Dedicated to My Brother Alvin Bryant and My Brother & True Friend Travis Stocking -4- Believing in Me When Everybody Turned Their Back! I'm Loyal -2- You Big Bro for Life.
Gladiator for Life!

When the Sunshine Turns-to-Rain

Day by day I search for the place to grow, to flow, to walk slow, to shake off the dirt and glow.
But something just won't let me go.
I can't tell you why, I just don't know. The sunshine turns to rain.
The pain turns to pain.
Nothing seems to change.
As I paint pictures inside my brain.
I wanna to cry but I can't.
I wanna to scream but I ain't .
I wanna to run but I fall.
I wanna to get back up and stand tall.
Where is my spirit, my soul, my flesh, my me.
Why come I can't be free.
I want the sunshine to let me hold it inside my hands.
I'm serious, I'll leave that thought as it stands. Take me and let me touch the air.
Oops nothings even there.
Oops watch out I tripped over the first step to that stair.
Who made the first chair
Who invented hair?
Who really cares, so much flair.
Damn my eraser made the paper tear.
Who hears my words, my voice, my choice,
My eyes are moist.
I don't know what I'm saying.
I'm serious I'm not playing.
Looking at the cigarette smoke float thru the sky.
Look at it with one eye.
Why do we cry? Die? Lie? Fly? Try? Buy? Wonder why?
Say hi? Then say goodbye!
Damn I want to touch the sky.
Who created me? Was it God? Please let me see.

Please let me be free.
Let me see how it was done. Was it fun?
Who made the gun?
Who made the sunshine the rain and the sun? Plant the seed
that I paint on this paper.
Cold caper don't rape her.
Reshape her, hem it, it needs a taper.
God was he the maker?
Or was he the caretaker.
What does these words mean?
Who created the dream? The coffee to the cream.
The cocaine to the triple bean.
The thing that made them scream.
The person who made the team.
What?
What is good or bad luck?
The bullet that made you duck?
The sun the moon, the rain, the brain that show the other
brain, create it, debate it, made it,
hate it, unrated, updated, underrated.
Try something new.
Mix red with blue.
Look at them their black I thought you knew.
Kill, heal, feel, real, deal, window seal, uncle bill.
The drug inside the pill, Jack and Jill.
The oil spill.
Who created the hill?
So much I want to know.
Go, Blow, throw.
Who Cares?
I laugh, smile, and think.
I drink,
My memory bank.
Sharpen the prison shank.
Put the fish in the tank.
Oh, my brain. Just went blank.
When the sunshine turns to rain.
So, tell me what you think.

I Miss You Momma
I Really Do!

I miss you mama I really do.
That's why I had to sit down and write this poem for you!
I saw your big, beautiful smile looking down from heaven
From up above.
Gosh mama I miss you, and I miss your one-of-a-kind love.
Last night mama my tears hit the floor.
Me and all your kids
We can't believe that we won't see you no more.
All I have is photo albums with pictures
Of your beautiful little face.
Why? Why? Did you save this place?
October 3rd my birthday you left this earth.
October 3rd on my birthday 57 years ago.
You gave me birth without you there wouldn't be us.
I miss you so much mama, my heart is about to burst.
Believe me I'm talking for real, trust for days and years I've
been walking in a trance.
My hands are holding my tears as I place another one/ Inside
the pockets of my pants.
I'm just trying to hold all of the memories
Of you inside my memory bank.
To believe that you are no longer here with us.
I still hear your voice and your wonderful laughter.
I have been asking God, every day, why did he allow your
life to end in 05 the 62nd chapter.
Your life has been a beautiful and interesting book to read.
But I'm searching for the rest of it, because this book about
you, is so cool, yes indeed.
Your life, your story, your body of life was the #1 best seller
of all time.

Gosh mama you know I miss you more than anything I am
not lying.
I wish our lives as human never had to come to an end.
Man, I wish I could push restart
And start yours all over again.
I've been trying to cope since I heard the tragic news.
As I write this poem sitting here my radio is playing and I'm
Listening to the blues.
I know you probably don't want me to do this at all.
Gosh I wish I could call you in heaven.
Boy that would be a beautiful phone call.
We would talk about so many different things.
We got a lot of new additions to the family tree.
Last night I trimmed the leaves and place these names.
When you first left I couldn't sleep, and I couldn't eat.
I couldn't even put a pair of shoes on my feet.
The while situation I just wanted to delete.
I want you back lord knows we all want you back.
To lose you mama is not a joke at all.
I'm talking to everybody, white, Asian, Mexican and Black.
Appreciate your mama every day,
Every hour and every minute that you have.
She is the most important leaf on the tree of life, she is all
The way legit.
She gave you the greatest gift ever.
She gave you life.
Mama if you needed my hear to live I would have cut it out
of my chest with a knife.
Right now, I find my brain rewinding back like a tape
recorder, saying seeing you as a little girl.
Gosh I wish I could bring you back
Right now today into this world.
I just want to once again hold your little hand and show you
how much I've grown up.

If you ever need us to do anything do us here on earth while
you're there in heaven.
Just call any of us your kids and family we will all answer
Your call twenty-four seven.
I still can see your last smile.
Last wave and hearing your last words
And even your last laugh.
We all had so much fun with you, it was so many memories,
We can't even add up all the math.
Well before I go I just want you to know that last night my
Tears once again hit the floor.
I'm still waiting, I just know you are going to walk back
Through that door.
Mama last night my tear hid the floor.
I miss you mama I really do.
That's so why I had to sit down and write this poem for you
Dedicated to and written for Yvonne James and the entire
Stocking Family.
We miss you mama we really do.

www.ingramcontent.com/pod-product-compliance
Lightning Source LLC
Chambersburg PA
CBHW051451290426
44109CB00016B/1712